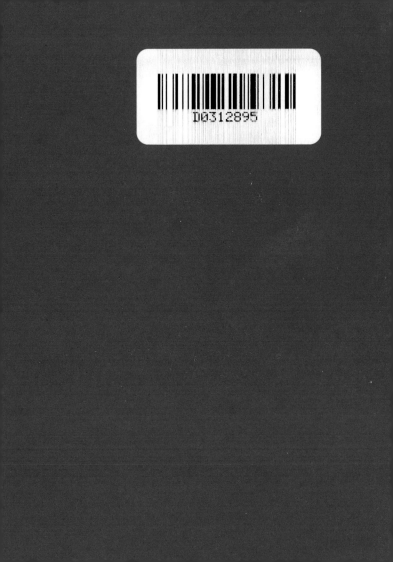

Sun Tzu's Art of War

# Sun Tzu's Art of War

**GENERAL TAO HANZHANG**

Translated by Yuan Shibing

The Modern Chinese Interpretation

STERLING
INNOVATION
A Division of Sterling Publishing Co., Inc
New York

Library of Congress Cataloging-in-Publication Data Available

10 9 8 7 6 5 4 3 2 1

Published in 2007 by Sterling Innovation, a division of
Sterling Publishing Company, Inc.
387 Park Avenue South, New York, N.Y. 10016
© 2000, 1987 by General Tao Hanzhang

Distributed in Canada by Sterling Publishing
c/o Canadian Manda Group, 165 Dufferin Street,
Toronto, Ontario, Canada M6K 3H6

Distributed in the United Kingdom by GMC Distribution Services,
Castle Place, 166 High Street, Lewes, East Sussex, England BN7 1XU

Distributed in Australia by Capricorn Link (Australia) Pty. Ltd.
P.O. Box 704, Windsor, NSW 2756, Australia

*Manufactured in China*
*All rights reserved*

Sterling ISBN-13: 978-1-4027-4552-2
ISBN-10: 1-4027-4552-4

For information about custom editions, special sales,
premium and corporate purchases, please contact Sterling Special Sales
Department at 800-805-5489 or specialsales@sterlingpub.com

Interior Design: Leah Lococo Ltd
Interior Illustrations: Monica Gurevich

# Contents

## The Hanzhang Interpretation
## Part I  101

## The Hanzhang Interpretation
## Part II  175

# Translator's Note

Sun Tzu's Art of War is a classical work on military affairs written approximately twenty-four hundred years ago. Although it is a military work, it is not confined to military affairs. Much of the text is also devoted to relationships between warfare and politics, economics, diplomacy, geography, and astronomy. It is, therefore, not surprising that Sun Tzu's Art of War is the only work of many written on the subject which has been handed down all through the ages, becoming popular abroad as well as in China.

The present book, Sun Tzu's Art of War: The Modern Chinese Interpretation, was written by General Tao Hanzhang, a senior officer in the Chinese People's Liberation Army (PLA). Born in 1917 in Jiangxi Province, China, General Tao joined the Red Army in 1933 and took part in the world-famous, arduous Long March in 1934–35. He fought in numerous battles during the Anti-Japanese War as a regimental commander and chief of staff of a brigade. During the Chinese Liberation War, he was chief of staff of an army. Later, he was the provost in the North China Military and Political College. Since the founding of the People's Republic of China, he has held many important military posts, such as the chief of staff of China's Kwangzhou Military Zone. General Tao has been a military educator in the PLA for many years, giving lectures and holding leading posts in China's highest military educational institution—the Chinese Military Academy.

Retired at the age of 68, General Tao serves as a senior adviser of the Beijing Institute for International Strategic Studies. He has visited the United States, Britain, France, and many other countries, lecturing on Chinese military thought and strategic problems. Out of the rich experiences of his military career, General Tao has published a number of works of theoretical and practical significance: *Military Operations in Tropical Jungles, The Work of a Staff Officer, The Work of Headquarters in Modern Warfare,* and several others.

In this book, his latest one, General Tao offers not only a vivid, clear, and analytical explanation of Sun Tzu's thought on the art of war, but also makes penetrating comments on its values and its shortcomings with an expert eye. In historical perspective, he also takes into consideration the development of modern weapons and technology. Written largely from the perspective of a Chinese military man who has been engaged in wars for most of his life, the book provides a comprehensive framework for approaching modern as well as ancient Chinese military thought. General Tao has combined *Sun Tzu's Art of War* with the theory of modern war. Considered in the light of present-day Chinese military theory, one finds both indications of change and aspects of continuity in this sphere.

General Tao's book treats the difficult subject of military theory in a simple language that is easily accessible to those who are not experts in military affairs. I believe this book will not only make interesting and instructive reading for those engaged in military, political, or foreign affairs, but will also help individuals develop their ability to make judgments and to synthesize and make decisions.

There are some discrepancies and deletions in translation with regard to quotations from *Sun Tzu's Art of War,* which appears in the Appendix, and General Tao's work (Parts I and II). This is the result of my endeavor to find the most exact terms for the original ancient Chinese. However, these discrepancies are insignificant, and none of them alters the true meaning of the text.

My thanks are extended to my friend, Dr. Derick Wilde, who read part of the manuscript and gave very useful advice on points of language.

YUAN SHIBING, Associate Professor
*Foreign Affairs College*
*Beijing, China*

# Introduction

**S**un Tzu's Art of War was written by Sun Tzu, the most famous military scientist and one of the ablest commanders in Ancient China. The exact dates of his birth and death are not known, but he lived around 500 B.C.; therefore, he was a contemporary of Confucius. According to *Shi Ji: The Biography of Wu Zixu,* Sun Tzu and his book of thirteen chapters on the art of war were recommended by General Wu Zixu to He Lu, the sovereign of the kingdom of Wu. Recognizing that Sun Tzu was very good at military affairs, He Lu appointed Sun Tzu a general in the kingdom.

*The Art of War,* written approximately 2,400 to 2,500 years ago, is the earliest and most complete book on the strategy of war available in China. The current book is somewhat different from what appears on the bamboo slips, the original *Sun Tzu's Art of War,* that were excavated from the Yingue Mountains. These bamboo slips date from the early years of the West Han Dynasty, about 350 years after the end of the Spring and Autumn Period (770–476 B.C.), which indicates three important points: 1) The time that *Sun Tzu's Art of War* was thought to be written is correct; 2) It is indeed Sun Tzu who wrote the book and not, as has been suggested, the writings of someone else in his name and; 3) The discrepancies between the content of the present edition of *Sun Tzu's Art of War* in circulation and what appears on the bamboo slips shows that this classic military work has been revised throughout different dynasties—new ideas being incorporated from the notations made as various renowned marshals and generals studied the work.

Actually, scarcely any Chinese generals throughout the ages studied *Sun Tzu's Art of War* without writing down their own comments and annotations. Famous among them are Sun Bin in the Warring States (475–221 B.C.), Zhang Liang and Han Xin in the West Han Dynasty, Zhuge Liang and Cao Cao in the Period of the Three Kingdoms, Li Shiming and Li Jing in the Tang Dynasty, Yue Fei and Li Gang in the Song Dynasty, Yeluchucai in the Yuan Dynasty, Liu Boweng in the Ming Dynasty and Zhen Guofang in the Qin Dynasty. Some even contributed unique and original ideas.

A number of contemporary marshals and generals in the People's Liberation Army of China are known to have thoroughly studied *Sun Tzu's Art of War*. Mao Zedong, for instance, praised the work highly, saying that Sun Tzu's doctrine, "Know the enemy and know yourself; in a hundred battles you will never be defeated," is scientifically true. Marshal Liu Bocheng studied *Sun Tzu's Art of War* so thoroughly he could even recite it, and he applied the book with great flexibility and proficiency. He personally translated one of the chapters, "Posture of Army," from classical to modern Chinese. Marshal Liu Bocheng's manuscript is still kept in military archives.

Many military experts and commanders in the People's Liberation Army drew on doctrines and principles in *Sun Tzu's Art of War* and applied them in many victorious battles under the guidance of Mao Zedong.

*Sun Tzu's Art of War* has been an important work of military science in world history, becoming well known abroad, too. Introduced into Japan in China's Tang Dynasty, it has been studied there quite widely since, much earlier and more extensively than in Europe and America. The book was considered the "Bible of Military Art," the "First *Art of War* in the World," and the "Originator of the Oriental Art of War."

It wasn't until sometime during the Qing Dynasty (1636–1911) that *Sun Tzu's Art of War* began to be known in Europe and was translated one after the other into English, French, German, Russian and Czech. Napoleon often studied the book while commanding battles. When William II, after having been defeated in World War I, came across the sentence in *Sun Tzu's Art of War* "A sovereign cannot launch a war because he is enraged, nor can a general fight a war because he is resentful," the German emperor sighed ruefully and said: "I should have read the book twenty years ago."

Decades after World War II, famed British military strategist Captain Sir Basil Liddell Hart wrote a foreword to a new English translation of *The Art of War*, saying: "There has long been need of a fresh and fuller translation of Sun Tzu, more adequately interpreting his thought. That need has increased with the development of nuclear weapons, potentially suicidal and genocidal."

John Collins, in his book *Grand Strategy, Practices and Principles,* stated: "The first great mind to shape strategic thought . . . belonged to Sun Tzu, who produced the earliest known treatise on the art of war sometime between 400 and 320 B.C. [sic]. His thirteen little essays rank with the best of all time, including those of Clausewitz, who wrote twenty-two centuries later. No one today has a firmer feel for strategic interrelationships, considerations, and constraints. Most of his ideas make just as much sense in our environment as they did in his."

A current U.S. Army publication on conducting military operations begins with Sun Tzu's famous advice, to "attack the enemy where he is most unprepared, and act when you are not expected."

Richard B. Foster, formerly in charge of a strategic studies center ("think tank") at Stanford Research Institute (now SRI International), and Japanese professor Osamu Miyoshi once proposed a new strategy to improve U.S. and Soviet "balance" in accordance with Sun Tzu's "offensive strategy." They named it "the nuclear strategy of Sun Tzu."

In the early 1960s, Field Marshal Bernard L. Montgomery of Great Britain said, during his visit to China, that a compulsory course on *Sun Tzu's Art of War* should be established in all the military academies throughout the world.

U.S. newspapers reported that the former U.S. commander in the Vietnam War, General William C. Westmoreland, quoted from *Sun Tzu's Art of War* "There has never been a protracted war which benefited a country" to prove his assertion that the United States should have withdrawn from that war earlier.

As early as 1888, the Department of General Staff of the Russian Army wrote articles systematically to introduce *Sun Tzu's Art of War*. During World War II, the Soviet Government, in response to a proposal from the Voroshilov Institute, translated *Sun Tzu's Art of War* directly from Chinese to Russian and listed it as an important course in the history of military science.

*Sun Tzu's Art of War* covers many areas, including the law of war, philosophy, strategic considerations, politics, economics, diplomacy, astronomy, and geography. The book should be studied from the modern point of view, selecting the essences and discarding the irrelevancies, making the past serve the present in order to develop it. Study of the book will greatly help military commanders at all levels in directing a war, organizing battles, developing wisdom, and increasing ability.

## MARSHAL LIU BOCHENG'S THEORIES ON SUN TZU

Marshal Liu Bocheng, the president of the Chinese Military Academy in the 1950s, once said that *Sun Tzu's Art of War* is a work of universal rules on guiding and commanding wars. It contains several marked features that make it unique compared to other books on the art of war.

**1.** It is an ancient work on universal laws of war. It is a profound exposition of factors leading to victory and to defeat, and stresses the importance of calculations (the final military decision before a war).

**2.** It stresses the relationship between war and such factors as politics, economics, diplomacy, astronomy, and geography. A commander is required to judge the hour, size up the situation and anticipate the enemy's decisions before launching or directing a war. He should never act rashly.

**3.** It emphasizes defeating one's enemy by strategic considerations, not by force.

**4.** It expresses the belief that "to subdue the enemy without fighting is the supreme excellence" in a war. That is to say, we should use comprehensive means—including political, diplomatic, economic, and technical resources instead of purely military means—to subdue the enemy.

**5.** It maintains that in a war one should adroitly guide military action and bring one's initiative into full play so as to lure the enemy onto the road to defeat.

**6.** It stresses that a commander must try his best to "bring the enemy to the battlefield and not to be brought there by him [the enemy]" whether in a strategic or tactical sense. The commander should, in any case, contend for the initiative, without which one is likely to be defeated or even annihilated.

**7.** It also stresses the importance of employing troops flexibly, according to the position and conditions of your enemy and yourself, and of topography.

**8.** It attaches great importance to "knowing your enemy and yourself" if you want to win a war. In present-day language, it means one must be realistic and practical and be certain about all situations before making the final decision to fight. Subjective assumption and rash action surely lead to defeat.

**9.** It advocates that employing troops must be unpredictable to the enemy and catch him by surprise. It stresses that when you attack, you must use overwhelming superiority, like a fierce tiger jumping upon a sheep, and when you want to end a battle, end it as suddenly as a flash of lightning.

As president of the Chinese Military Academy in the 1950s, Marshal Liu Bocheng strongly held that *Sun Tzu's Art of War* should be the main textbook for the course entitled "Science of Campaigns," which he himself taught. Liu Bocheng also sponsored a symposium on the book at the Military Academy. While his lectures were not limited to the book itself, he drew the essence from the book and summarized it in the following six points:

1. Strategic considerations
2. Posture of army
3. Extraordinary and normal forces
4. Void and actuality
5. Initiative and flexibility in employing troops
6. Use of spies

Marshal Liu brilliantly cited a large number of battles, stories, personal experiences, and other examples to elaborate on law, philosophy, and strategies of war in simple terms.

This present book has been written from my own study of *Sun Tzu's Art of War* with reference to the file of the symposium and the book *Posture of Army*, which Marshal Liu translated and revised from the classic Chinese.

## THE VALIDITY OF
## SUN TZU'S DOCTRINE

In ancient times, many Chinese generals wrote on the art of war. According to *The History of Sung Dynasty*, besides *Sun Tzu's Art of War* were such well-known works as: *Wu Tzu's Art of War*, *The Six Points of Military Strategy*, *The Three Stratagems* by Huang Shi Gong *Wei Liao Zi*, *The Law of Sima*, and *The Dialogue between Emperor Tang Taizhong and Li Wei Gong*. Many of these writings are obsolete today, with only a few still accessible somewhere in the world. None ever gained the popularity of *Sun Tzu's Art of War*—which shows the vitality and practical value of Sun Tzu's doctrine.

In directing a modern war or making final decisions, it is of practical significance for us to study *Sun Tzu's Art of War*. This modern interpretation evoked wide public interest and attention both at home, when first published in Chinese in 1985, and abroad, when it was published in English in New York in 1987.

*Sun Tzu's Art of War* is an extremely valuable asset handed down by our ancestors. It is essential for us to reject both dogmatism and conservatism during the process of our study. At the same time, we should also adapt ourselves to the times so that we can develop a universal art of war.

# Sun Tzu's Art of War

The original text

# Chapter 1
## Estimates

War is a matter of vital importance to the state; a matter of life or death, the road either to survival or to ruin. Hence, it is imperative that it be studied thoroughly.

Therefore, appraise it in terms of the five fundamental factors and make comparisons of the various conditions of the antagonistic sides in order to ascertain the results of a war. The first of these factors is politics; the second, weather; the third, terrain; the fourth, the commander; and the fifth, doctrine. Politics means the thing which causes the people to be in harmony with their ruler so that they will follow him in disregard of their lives and without fear of any danger. Weather signifies night and day, cold and heat, fine days and rain, and change of seasons. Terrain means distances, and refers to whether the ground is traversed with ease or difficulty and to whether it is open or constricted, and influences your chances of life or death. The commander stands for the general's qualities of wisdom, sincerity, benevolence, courage, and strictness. Doctrine is to be understood as the organization of the army, the gradations of rank among the officers, the regulation of supply routes, and the provision of military materials to the army.

These five fundamental factors are familiar to every general. Those who master them win; those who do not are defeated. Therefore, in laying plans, compare the following seven elements, appraising them with the utmost care.

**1.** Which ruler is wise and more able?

**2.** Which commander is more talented?

**3.** Which army obtains the advantages of nature and the terrain?

**4.** In which army are regulations and instructions better carried out?

**5.** Which troops are stronger?

**6.** Which army has the better trained officers and men?

**7.** Which army administers rewards and punishments in a more enlightened and correct way?

By means of these seven elements, I shall be able to forecast which side will be victorious and which will be defeated.

The general who heeds my counsel is sure to win. Such a general should be retained in command. One who ignores my counsel is certain to be defeated. Such a one should be dismissed.

Having paid attention to my counsel and plans, the general must create a situation which will contribute to their accomplishment. By "situation" I mean he should take the field situation into consideration and act in accordance with what is advantageous.

All warfare is based on deception. Therefore, when capable of attacking, feign incapacity; when active in moving troops, feign inactivity. When near the enemy, make it seem that you are far away; when far away, make it seem that you are near. Hold out baits to lure the enemy. Strike the enemy when he is in disorder. Prepare against the enemy when he is secure at all points. Avoid the enemy for the time being when he is stronger. If your opponent is of choleric temper, try to irritate him. If he is arrogant, try to encourage his egotism. If the enemy troops are well prepared after reorganization, try to wear them down. If they are united, try to sow dissension among them. Attack the enemy where he is unprepared, and appear where you are not expected. These are the keys to victory for a strategist. It is not possible to formulate them in detail beforehand.

Now, if the estimates made before a battle indicate victory, it is because careful calculations show that your conditions are more favorable than those of your enemy; if they indicate defeat, it is because careful calculations show that favorable conditions for a battle are fewer. With more careful calculations, one can win; with less, one cannot. How much less chance of victory has one who makes no calculations at all! By this means, one can foresee the outcome of a battle.

# For Further Thought

Sun Tzu elaborates on deceptions used in battle, to ensure opportune circumstances. Use this space to find modern applications for this strategy. List possible circumstances in your professional or personal environments that can be taken advantage of in pursuit of victory.

# Chapter 2
# Waging War

In operations of war—when one thousand fast four-horse chariots, one thousand heavy chariots, and one thousand mail-clad soldiers are required; when provisions are transported for a thousand *li*; when there are expenditures at home and at the front, and stipends for entertainment of envoys and advisers—the cost of materials such as glue and lacquer, and of chariots and armor, will amount to one thousand pieces of gold a day. One hundred thousand troops may be dispatched only when this money is in hand.

A speedy victory is the main object in war. If this is long in coming, weapons are blunted and morale depressed. If troops are attacking cities, their strength will be exhausted. When the army engages in protracted campaigns, the resources of the state will fall short. When your weapons are dulled and ardor dampened, your strength exhausted and treasure spent, the chieftains of the neighboring states will take advantage of your crisis to act. In that case, no man, however wise, will be able to avert the disastrous consequences that ensue. Thus, while we have heard of stupid haste in war, we have not yet seen a clever operation that was prolonged. For there has never been a protracted war which benefited a country. Therefore, those unable to understand the evils inherent in employing troops are equally unable to understand the advantageous ways of doing so.

Those adept in waging war do not require a second levy of conscripts or more than two provisionings. They carry military equipment from the homeland, but rely on the enemy for provisions. Thus, the army is plentifully provided with food.

When a country is impoverished by military operations, it is due to distant transportation; carrying supplies for great distances renders the people destitute. Where troops are gathered, prices go up. When prices rise, the wealth of the people is drained away. When wealth is drained away, the people will be afflicted with urgent and heavy exactions. With this loss of wealth and exhaustion of strength, the households in the country will be extremely poor and seven-tenths of their wealth dissipated. As to government expenditures, those due to broken-down chariots, worn-out horses, armor and helmets, bows and arrows, spears and shields, protective mantlets, draft oxen, and wagons will amount to 60 percent of the total.

Hence, a wise general sees to it that his troops feed on the enemy, for one *zhong* of the enemy's provisions is equivalent to twenty of one's own and one *shi* of the enemy's fodder to twenty *shi* of one's own.

In order to make the soldiers courageous in overcoming the enemy, they must be roused to anger. In order to capture more booty from the enemy, soldiers must have their rewards.

Therefore, in chariot fighting when more than ten chariots are captured, reward those who take the first. Replace the enemy's flags and banners with your own, mix the captured chariots with yours, and mount them. Treat the prisoners of war well, and care for them. This is called "winning a battle and becoming stronger."

Hence, what is valued in war is victory, not prolonged operations. And the general who understands how to employ troops is the minister of the people's fate and arbiter of the nation's destiny.

# For Further Thought

Sun Tzu speaks of swift operations as a necessary component of victory. Use this space to reflect upon previous personal or professional battles that have overextended your resources as a result of their extended duration. If the battle itself left you vulnerable to defeat, how might you have ended it sooner?

# Chapter 3
# Offensive Strategy

Generally, in war the best policy is to take a state intact; to ruin it is inferior to this. To capture the enemy's entire army is better than to destroy it; to take intact a regiment, a company, or a squad is better than to destroy them. [Regiment, company, and squad are *lu, zu,* and *wu* in Chinese. In ancient China, five hundred soldiers made up a *lu,* one hundred a *zu,* and five a *wu.*] For to win one hundred victories in one hundred battles is not the acme of skill. To subdue the enemy without fighting is the supreme excellence.

Thus, what is of supreme importance in war is to attack the enemy's strategy. Next best is to disrupt his alliances by diplomacy. The next best is to attack his army. And the worst policy is to attack cities. Attack cities only when there is no alternative because to prepare big shields and wagons and make ready the necessary arms and equipment require at least three months, and to pile up earthen ramps against the walls requires an additional three months. The general, unable to control his impatience, will order his troops to swarm up the wall like ants, with the result that one-third of them will be killed without taking the city. Such is the calamity of attacking cities.

Thus, those skilled in war subdue the enemy's army without battle. They capture the enemy's cities without assaulting them and overthrow his state without protracted operations. Their aim is to take all under heaven intact by strategic considerations. Thus, their troops are not worn out and their gains will be complete. This is the art of offensive strategy.

Consequently, the art of using troops is this: When ten to the enemy's one, surround him. When five times his strength, attack him. If double his strength, divide him. If equally matched, you may engage him with some good plan. If weaker numerically, be capable of withdrawing. And if in all respects unequal, be capable of eluding him, for a small force is but booty for one more powerful if it fights recklessly.

Now, the general is the assistant to the sovereign of the

state. If this assistance is all-embracing, the state will surely be strong; if defective, the state will certainly be weak.

Now, there are three ways in which a sovereign can bring misfortune upon his army:

**1.** When ignorant that the army should not advance, to order an advance; or when ignorant that it should not retire, to order a retirement. This is described as "hobbling the army."

**2.** When ignorant of military affairs, to interfere in their administration. This causes the officers to be perplexed.

**3.** When ignorant of command problems, to interfere with the direction of fighting. This engenders doubts in the minds of the officers.

If the army is confused and suspicious, neighboring rulers will take advantage of this and cause trouble. This is what is meant by: "A confused army leads to another's victory."

Thus, there are five points in which victory may be predicted:

**1.** He who knows when he can fight and when he cannot will be victorious.

**2.** He who understands how to fight in accordance with the strength of antagonistic forces will be victorious.

**3.** He whose ranks are united in purpose will be victorious.

**4.** He who is well prepared and lies in wait for an enemy who is not well prepared will be victorious.

**5.** He whose generals are able and not interfered with by the sovereign will be victorious.

**It is in these five matters that the way to victory is known.**

**Therefore, I say:** Know the enemy and know yourself; in a hundred battles, you will never be defeated. When you are ignorant of the enemy but know yourself, your chances of winning or losing are equal. If ignorant both of your enemy and of yourself, you are sure to be defeated in every battle.

# For Further Thought

If it is the "supreme excellence" to "subdue the enemy without fighting," and "the worst policy is to attack cities," how does this apply to twenty-first century living? In personal battles, regardless of the arena, "attacking cities" can be seen as the equivalent of personal attacks or confrontations where exposure creates vulnerability. Use this space to not only reflect upon previous conflicts in which your approach has left you vulnerable solely as a result of your participation, but also what steps could have been taken to avoid these situations while still gaining an overall advantage.

_____

_____

_____

_____

_____

_____

_____

# Chapter 4
# Dispositions

The skillful warriors in ancient times first made themselves invincible and then awaited the enemy's moment of vulnerability. Invincibility depends on oneself, but the enemy's vulnerability on himself. It follows that those skilled in war can make themselves invincible but cannot cause an enemy to be certainly vulnerable. Therefore, it can be said that, one may know how to win, but cannot necessarily do so.

Defend yourself when you cannot defeat the enemy, and attack the enemy when you can. One defends when his strength is inadequate; he attacks when it is abundant. Those who are skilled in defense hide themselves as under the nine-fold earth [In ancient China, the number nine was used to signify the highest number.]; those in attack flash forth as from above the ninefold heavens. Thus, they are capable both of protecting themselves and of gaining a complete victory.

To foresee a victory which the ordinary man can foresee is not the acme of excellence. Neither is it if you triumph in battle and are universally acclaimed "expert," for to lift an autumn down requires no great strength, to distinguish between the sun and moon is no test of vision, to hear the thunderclap is no indication of acute hearing. In ancient times, those called skilled in war conquered an enemy easily conquered. And, therefore, the victories won by a master of war gain him neither reputation for wisdom nor merit for courage. For he wins his victories without erring. Without erring he establishes the certainty of his victory; he conquers an enemy already defeated. Therefore, the skillful commander takes up a position in which he cannot be defeated and misses no opportunity to overcome his enemy. Thus, a victorious army always seeks battle after his plans indicate that victory is possible under them, whereas an army destined to defeat fights in the hope of winning but without any planning. Those skilled in war cultivate their policies and strictly adhere to the laws and regulations. Thus, it is in their power to achieve success.

Now, the elements of the art of war are first, the measurement of space; second, the estimation of quantities; third, calculations; fourth, comparisons; and fifth, chances of victory. Measurements of space are derived from the ground. Quantities derive from measurement, figures from quantities, comparisons from figures, and victory from comparisons. Thus, a victorious army is as one *yi* [an ancient Chinese weight, approximately equivalent to 24 ounces] balanced against a grain, and a defeated army is as a grain balanced against one *yi*.

It is because of disposition that a victorious general is able to make his soldiers fight with the effect of pent-up waters which, suddenly released, plunge into a bottomless abyss.

# For Further Thought

Sun Tzu's writing on disposition reveals many of his views on planning and leadership. Use this space to either reflect on your own performance as a leader while preparing for a specific challenge, or to analyze the role played by those who have led you through an arduous task.

# Chapter 5
# Posture of Army

Generally, management of a large force is the same as management of a few men. It is a matter of organization. And to direct a large force is the same as to direct a few men. This is a matter of formations and signals. That the army is certain to sustain the enemy's attack without suffering defeat is due to operations of the extraordinary and the normal forces. Troops thrown against the enemy as a grindstone against eggs is an example of a solid acting upon a void.

Generally, in battle, use the normal force to engage and use the extraordinary to win. Now, the resources of those skilled in the use of extraordinary forces are as infinite as the heavens and earth, as inexhaustible as the flow of the great rivers, for they end and recommence—cyclical, as are the movements of the sun and moon. They die away and are reborn—recurrent, as are the passing seasons. The musical notes are only five in number, but their combination gives rise to so many melodies that one cannot hear them all. The primary colors are only five in number, but their combinations are so infinite that one cannot visualize them all. The flavors are only five in number, but their blends are so various that one cannot taste them all. In battle, there are only the normal and extraordinary forces, but their combinations are limitless; none can comprehend them all. For these two forces are mutually reproductive. It is like moving in an endless circle. Who can exhaust the possibilities of their combination?

When torrential water tosses boulders, it is because of its momentum; when the strike of a hawk breaks the body of its prey, it is because of timing. Thus, the momentum of one skilled in war is overwhelming, and his attack precisely timed. His potential is that of a fully drawn crossbow; his timing, that of the release of the trigger.

In the tumult and uproar, the battle seems chaotic, but there must be no disorder in one's own troops. The battlefield may seem in confusion and chaos, but one's array must be in good order. That will be proof against defeat. Apparent confusion is a product of good order; apparent cowardice, of courage; apparent weakness, of strength. Order or disorder depends on organization and direction; courage or cowardice on circumstances; strength or weakness on tactical dispositions. Thus, one who is skilled at making the enemy move does so by creating a situation, according to which the enemy will act. He entices the enemy with something he is certain to want. He keeps the enemy on the move by holding out bait and then attacks him with picked troops.

Therefore, a skilled commander seeks victory from the situation and does not demand it of his subordinates. He selects suitable men and exploits the situation. He who utilizes the situation uses his men in fighting as one rolls logs or stones. Now, the nature of logs and stones is that on stable ground they are static; on a slope, they move. If square, they stop; if round, they roll. Thus, the energy of troops skillfully commanded in battle may be compared to the momentum of round boulders which roll down from a mountain thousands of feet in height.

# For Further Thought

Sun Tzu writes of managing forces as a process by which one gets the greatest potential from their resources. His remarks on the normal and extraordinary relate to the utilization of strengths. Use the space below to list your strengths or the strengths of those you manage, and reflect as to how they are being used, and what might be done to take fuller advantage of them.

# Chapter 6
# Void and Actuality

Generally, he who occupies the field of battle first and awaits his enemy is at ease, and he who comes later to the scene and rushes into the fight is weary. And, therefore, those skilled in war bring the enemy to the field of battle and are not brought there by him. **One able to make the enemy come of his own accord does so by offering him some advantage. And one able to stop him from coming does so by preventing him. Thus,** when the enemy is at ease be able to tire him, when well fed to starve him, when at rest to make him move.

Appear at places which he is unable to rescue; move swiftly in a direction where you are least expected.

That you may march a thousand *li* without tiring yourself is because you travel where there is no enemy. To be certain to take what you attack is to attack a place the enemy does not or cannot protect. To be certain to hold what you defend is to defend a place the enemy dares not or is not able to attack. Therefore, against those skilled in attack, the enemy does not know where to defend, and against the experts in defense, the enemy does not know where to attack.

How subtle and insubstantial, that the expert leaves no trace. How divinely mysterious, that he is inaudible. Thus, he is master of his enemy's fate. His offensive will be irresistible if he makes for his enemy's weak positions; he cannot be overtaken when he withdraws if he moves swiftly. When I wish to give battle, my enemy, even though protected by high walls and deep moats, cannot help but engage me, for I attack a position he must relieve. When I wish to avoid battle, I may defend myself simply by drawing a line on the ground; the enemy will be unable to attack me because I divert him from going where he wishes.

If I am able to determine the enemy's dispositions while, at the same time, I conceal my own, then I can concentrate my forces and his must be divided. And if I concentrate while he divides, I can use my entire strength to attack a fraction of his. Therefore, I will be numerically superior. Then, if I am able to use many to strike few at the selected point, those I deal with will fall into hopeless straits. The enemy must not know where I intend to give battle. For if he does not know where I intend to give battle, he must prepare in a great many places. And when he prepares in a great many places, those I have to fight in will be few. For if he prepares to the front, his rear will be weak, and if to the rear, his front will be fragile. If he strengthens his left, his right will be vulnerable, and if his right, there will be few troops on his left. And when he sends troops everywhere, he will be weak everywhere. Numerical weakness comes from having to guard against possible attacks; numerical strength from forcing the enemy to make these preparations against us.

If one knows where and when a battle will be fought, his troops can march a thousand *li* and meet on the field. But if one knows neither the battleground nor the day of battle, the left will be unable to aid the right and the right will be unable to aid the left, and the van will be unable to support the rear and the rear, the van. How much more is this so when separated by several tens of *li* or, indeed, by even a few! Although I estimate the troops of Yüe as many, of what benefit is this superiority with respect to the outcome of war? Thus, I say that victory can be achieved. For even if the enemy is numerically stronger, I can prevent him from engaging.

Therefore, analyze the enemy's plans so that you will know his shortcomings as well as strong points. Agitate him in order to ascertain the pattern of his movement. Lure him out to reveal his dispositions and ascertain his position. Launch a probing attack in order to learn where his strength is abundant and where deficient. The ultimate in disposing one's troops is to conceal them without ascertainable shape. **Then the most penetrating spies cannot pry nor can the wise lay plans against you. It is according to the situations that plans are laid for victory, but the multitude does not comprehend this. Although everyone can see the outward aspects, none understands how the victory is achieved. Therefore, when a victory is won, one's tactics are not repeated.** One should always respond to circumstances in an infinite variety of ways.

Now, an army may be likened to water, for just as flowing water avoids the heights and hastens to the lowlands, so an army should avoid strength and strike weakness. And as water shapes its flow in accordance with the ground, so an army manages its victory in accordance with the situation of the enemy. And as water has no constant form, there are in warfare no constant conditions. **Thus, one able to win the victory by modifying his tactics in accordance with the enemy situation may be said to be divine.** Of the five elements [water, fire, metal, wood, and earth], each may predominate; of the four seasons, none lasts forever; of the days, some are long and some short, and the moon waxes and wanes. That is also the law of employing troops.

# For Further Thought

Use this space to reflect upon an adversary. List their strengths and weaknesses, as well as the methods they traditionally employ to antagonize you. Include in your profile previous experiences where you have provoked them, and reflect upon their reactions.

_____

_____

_____

_____

_____

_____

_____

_____

_____

_____

_____

_____

_____

_____

# Chapter 7
# Maneuvering

Normally, in war, the general receives his commands from the sovereign. During the process from assembling the troops and mobilizing the people to blending the army into a harmonious entity and encamping it, nothing is more difficult than the art of maneuvering for advantageous positions. What is difficult about it is to make the devious route the most direct and to turn disadvantage to advantage. Thus, march by an indirect route and divert the enemy by enticing him with a bait. So doing, you may set out after he does and arrive at the battlefield before him. One able to do this shows the knowledge of the artifice of diversion.

Therefore, both advantage and danger are inherent in maneuvering for an advantageous position. One who sets the entire army in motion with impediments to pursue an advantageous position will not attain it. If he abandons the camp and all the impediments to contend for advantage, the stores will be lost. Thus, if one orders his men to make forced marches without armor, stopping neither day nor night, covering double the usual distance at a stretch, and doing a hundred *li* to wrest an advantage, it is probable that the commanders will be captured. The stronger men will arrive first and the feeble ones will struggle along behind; so, if this method is used, only one-tenth of the army will reach its destination. In a forced march of fifty *li*, the commander of the van will probably fall, but half the army will arrive. In a forced march of thirty *li*, just two-thirds will arrive. It follows that an army which lacks heavy equipment, fodder, food, and stores will be lost.

One who is not acquainted with the designs of his neighbors should not enter into alliances with them. Those who do not know the conditions of mountains and forests, hazardous defiles, marshes and swamps, cannot conduct the march of an army. Those who do not use local guides are unable to obtain the advantages of the ground. Now, war is based on deception. Move when it is advantageous and create changes in the situation by dispersal and concentration of forces. When campaigning, be swift as the wind; in leisurely marching, majestic as the forest; in raiding and plundering, be fierce as fire; in standing, firm as the mountains. When hiding, be as unfathomable as things behind the clouds; when moving, fall like a thunderbolt. When you plunder the countryside, divide your forces. When you conquer territory, defend strategic points. Weigh the situation before you move. He who knows the artifice of diversion will be victorious. Such is the art of maneuvering.

*The Book of Military Administration* says: "As the voice cannot be heard in battle, drums and gongs are used. As troops cannot see each other clearly in battle, flags and banners are used." Now, gongs and drums, banners and flags are used to unify the action of the troops. When the troops can be thus united, the brave cannot advance alone, nor can the cowardly withdraw. This is the art of directing large masses of troops. In night fighting, use many torches and drums, in day fighting, many banners and flags, in order to guide the sight and hearing of our troops.

Now, an army may be robbed of its spirit and its commander deprived of his confidence. At the beginning of a campaign, the spirits of soldiers are keen; after a certain period of time, they flag; and in the later stage thoughts turn towards home. And therefore, those skilled in war avoid the enemy when his spirit is keen and attack him when it is sluggish and his soldiers are homesick. **This is the art of controlling the moral factor.** In good order, they await a disorderly enemy; in serenity, a clamorous one. This is the art of controlling the mental factor. Close to the field of battle, they await an enemy coming from afar; at rest, they await an exhausted enemy; with well-fed troops, they await hungry ones. This is the art of controlling the physical factor. They do not engage an enemy advancing with well-ordered banners nor one whose formations are in impressive array. This is the art of changing with the circumstances.

Therefore, the art of employing troops is that when the enemy occupies high ground, do not confront him uphill, and when his back is resting on hills, do not make a frontal attack. When he pretends to flee, do not pursue. Do not attack troops whose spirits are keen. Do not swallow bait. Do not thwart an enemy who is returning homewards.

Leave a way of escape to a surrounded enemy, and do not press a desperate enemy too hard. Such is the art of employing troops.

# For Further Thought

Sun Tzu discusses maneuvering and timing in the same breath. By his criteria, use this space to project possible events from which your adversary will be weakest.

---

# Chapter 8
# The Nine Variables

In general, the system of employing troops is that the commander receives his mandate from the sovereign to mobilize the people and assemble the army.

You should not encamp on grounds hard to approach. Unite with your allies on grounds intersected with highways. Do not linger on desolate ground. In enclosed ground, resort to strategem. In death ground, fight a last-ditch battle.

There are some roads which must not be followed, some troops which must not be attacked, some cities which must not be assaulted, and some ground which should not be contested. There are also occasions when the commands of the sovereign need not be obeyed. Therefore, a general thoroughly versed in the advantages of the nine variable factors knows how to employ troops. One who does not understand their advantages will not be able to use the terrain to his advantage even though he is well acquainted with it. In the direction of military operations, one who does not understand the tactics suitable to the nine variable situations will be unable to use his troops effectively, even if he understands the "five advantages" [referring to the five situations mentioned at the beginning of this paragraph].

And for this reason, a wise general in his deliberations must consider both favorable and unfavorable factors. By taking into account the favorable factors, he makes his plan feasible; by taking into account the unfavorable, he may avoid possible disasters.

He who wants to subdue dukes in neighboring states does so by inflicting injury upon them. He who wants to control them does so by keeping them constantly occupied, and he who makes them rush about does so by offering them ostensible advantages.

It is a doctrine of war not to assume the enemy will not come but rather to rely on one's readiness to meet him, and not to presume that he will not attack but rather to make oneself invincible.

There are five qualities which are fatal in the character of a general: If reckless, he can be killed; if cowardly, captured; if quick-tempered, he can be provoked to rage and make a fool of himself; if he has too delicate a sense of honor, he can be easily insulted; if he is of a compassionate nature, you can harass him.

Now these five traits of character are serious faults in a general and in military operations are calamitous. The ruin of the army and the death of the general are inevitable results of these shortcomings. They must be deeply pondered.

# For Further Thought

Use this space to weigh the favorable and unfavorable factors that will influence a decision or course of action that must be executed.

_____

_____

_____

_____

_____

_____

_____

_____

_____

_____

_____

_____

_____

_____

_____

# Chapter 9
# On the March

When an army takes up a position and confronts the enemy, it has to observe and judge the enemy situation. In doing so, it should pay attention to the following:

When crossing the mountains, be sure to stay close to valleys; when encamping, select high ground facing the sunny side; when high ground is occupied by the enemy, do not ascend to attack. So much for taking a position in mountains.

After crossing a river, you must move some distance away from it. When an advancing enemy crosses water, do not meet him in midstream. It is advantageous to allow half his force to tous torrents such as "heavenly wells," "heavenly prisons," "heavenly nets," "heavenly traps," and "heavenly cracks"—you must march speedily away from them. Do not approach them. Keep a distance from them and draw the enemy towards them. Face them and cause the enemy to put his back to them. When, on the flanks of the army, there are dangerous defiles or ponds covered with aquatic grasses where reeds and rushes grow, or forested mountains with dense tangled undergrowth, you must carefully search them out, for these are places where ambushes are laid and spies are hidden.

When the enemy is nearby but remains calm, he is depending on a favorable position. When he challenges battle from afar, he wishes to lure you to advance; when he is on easy ground, he must be in an advantageous position. When the trees are seen to move, it means the enemy is advancing. When many screens have been placed in the undergrowth, it is for the purpose of deception. Birds rising in flight are a sign that the enemy is lying in ambush; when the wild animals are startled and flee, the enemy is trying to take you unawares.

Dust spurting upwards in high straight columns indicates the approach of chariots. When it hangs low and is widespread, it betokens that infantry is approaching. When dust rises in scattered areas, the enemy is collecting and bringing in firewood; when there are numerous small patches which seem to come and go, he is encamping the army. When the enemy's envoys speak in humble terms, but the army continues preparations, that means it will advance. When their language is strong and the enemy pretentiously advances, these may be signs that the enemy will retreat. When light chariots first go out and take position on the flanks, the enemy is forming. When without a previous understanding the enemy asks for a truce, he must be plotting. When his troops march speedily and he parades his battle chariots, he is expecting to rendezvous with reinforcements. When half his force advances and half withdraws, he is attempting to decoy you. When his troops lean on their weapons, they are famished. When drawers of water drink before carrying it to camp, his troops are suffering from thirst. When the enemy sees an advantage but does not advance to seize it, he is fatigued. When birds gather above the enemy's campsites, they are unoccupied. When at night the enemy's camp is clamorous, it betokens nervousness.

When his troops are disorderly, the general has no prestige. When his flags and banners are shifted about constantly, he is in disarray. If the officers are short-tempered, they are exhausted. When the enemy feeds grain to the horses and kills its cattle for food, and when his troops neither hang up their cooking pots nor return to their shelters, the enemy is desperate. When the troops continually gather in small groups and whisper together, the general has lost the confidence of the army. Too frequent rewards indicate that the general is at the end of his resources; too frequent punishments that he is in acute distress. If the officers at first treat the men violently and later are fearful of them, it shows supreme lack of intelligence. **When the enemy's troops march up angrily and, although facing you, neither join battle for a long time nor leave, the situation requires great vigilance and thorough investigation.**

In war, numbers alone confer no advantage. **It is sufficient if you do not advance relying on sheer military power. If you estimate the enemy situation correctly and then concentrate your strength to overcome the enemy, there is no more to it than this.** He who lacks foresight and underestimates his enemy will surely be captured by him.

If troops are punished before their loyalty is secured, they will be disobedient. If not obedient, it is difficult to employ them. If troops have become attached to you, but discipline cannot be enforced, you cannot employ them. Thus, command them with civility but keep them under control by iron discipline, and it may be said that victory is certain. If orders are consistently carried out to instruct the troops, they will be obedient. If orders are not consistently carried out to instruct them, they will be disobedient.

If orders are consistently trustworthy and carried out, it shows that the relationship of a commander with his troops is satisfactory.

# For Further Thought

Sun Tzu spends time interpreting how troop behavior is an indicator of a leader's status and strength. Reflect upon your own command structure, as either a subordinate or a manager, and apply Sun Tzu's observations of his troops to the behavior of your personal or professional colleagues.

# Chapter 10
# Terrain

Ground may be classified according to its nature as accessible, entangling, temporizing, precipitous, distant, or having narrow passes. Ground which both we and the enemy can traverse with equal ease is called accessible. On such ground, he who first takes high sunny positions, and keeps his supply routes unimpeded can fight advantageously. Ground easy to reach but difficult to get out of is called entangling. The nature of this ground is such that if the enemy is unprepared and you sally out, you may defeat him. If the enemy is prepared and you sally out, but do not win, and it is difficult for you to return, it is unprofitable. Ground equally disadvantageous for both the enemy and ourselves to enter is called temporizing. The nature of this ground is such that although the enemy holds out a bait, I do not go forth but entice him by marching off. When I have drawn out half his force, I can strike him advantageously. If I first occupy narrow passes, I must block the passes and await the enemy. If the enemy first occupies such ground and blocks the defiles, I should not attack him; if he does not block them completely, I may do so. On precipitous ground, I must take a position on the sunny heights and await the enemy. If he first occupies such ground, I march off; I do not attack him. When at a distance from an enemy of equal strength, it is difficult to provoke battle and unprofitable to engage him.

These are the principles relating to six different types of ground. It is the highest responsibility of the general to inquire into them with the utmost care.

There are six conditions in which troops fail. These are: flight, insubordination, collapse in disorder, distress, disorganization, and rout. None of these disasters can be attributed to natural causes, but to the fault of the general.

Other conditions being equal, if a force attacks one ten times its size, the result is flight. When soldiers are strong and officers weak, the army is insubordinate. When the officers are valiant and the soldiers ineffective, the result is collapse. When officers are angry and insubordinate, and on encountering the enemy rush into battle with no understanding of the feasibility of engaging and without awaiting orders from the commander, the army is in distress. When the general is morally weak and without authority, when his instructions and guidance are not enlightened, when there are no consistent rules to guide the officers and men, and when the formations are slovenly, the result is disorganization. When a commander unable to estimate his enemy uses a small force to engage a large one, or weak troops to strike the strong, or when he fails to select shock troops for the van, the result is rout. When any of these six conditions prevails, the army is on the road to defeat. It is the highest responsibility of the general that he examine them carefully.

Conformation of the ground is of the greatest assistance in battle. Therefore, virtues of a superior general are to estimate the enemy situation and to calculate distances and the degree of difficulty of the terrain so as to obtain victory. He who fights with full knowledge of these factors is certain to win; he who does not will surely be defeated. If the situation is one of victory, but the sovereign has issued orders not to engage, the general may decide to fight. If the situation is such that he cannot win, but the sovereign has issued orders to engage, he need not do so. And, therefore, the general who in advancing does not seek personal fame, and in retreating is not concerned with disgrace, but whose only purpose is to protect the country and promote the best interests of his sovereign, is the precious jewel of the state.

A general regards his men as infants who will march with him into the deepest valleys. He treats them as his own beloved sons and they will stand by him unto death. If a general indulges his men but is unable to employ them, if he loves them but cannot enforce his commands, if the men are disorderly and he is unable to control them, they may be compared to spoiled children, and are useless.

If I know that my troops are capable of striking the enemy, but do not know that he is invulnerable to attack, my chance of victory is but half. If I know that the enemy is vulnerable to attack, but do not know that my troops are incapable of striking him, my chance of victory is but half. If I know that the enemy can be attacked and that my troops are capable of attacking him, but do not realize that the conformation of the ground makes fighting impracticable, my chance of victory is but half. Therefore, when those experienced in war move, they are never bewildered; when they act, their resources are limitless. And, therefore, I say: Know the enemy, know yourself; your victory will never be endangered. Know the ground, know the weather; your victory will then be complete.

# For Further Thought

Sun Tzu reflects upon the qualities of leadership, and provides critical assessment of both detrimental and valued traits. Engage in the same exercise with regards to the leaders that influence your life.

_____

_____

_____

_____

_____

_____

_____

_____

_____

_____

_____

_____

_____

# Chapter 11
# The Nine Varieties of Ground

In respect to the employment of troops, ground may be classified as dispersive, frontier, key, open, focal, serious, difficult, encircled, and desperate.

When a feudal lord fights in his own territory, he is in dispersive ground. When he makes but a shallow penetration into enemy territory, he is in frontier ground. Ground equally advantageous to occupy is key ground. Ground equally accessible is open. When a state is enclosed by three other states, its territory is focal. He who first gets control of it will gain the support of the majority of neighboring states. When the army has penetrated deep into hostile territory, leaving far behind many enemy cities and towns, it is in serious ground. When the army traverses mountains, forests, or precipitous country, or marches through defiles, marshlands, or swamps, or any place where the going is hard, it is in difficult ground. Ground to which access is constricted, where the way out is tortuous, and where a small enemy force can strike a larger one is called encircled. Ground in which the army survives only if it fights with the courage of desperation is called desperate. And, therefore, do not fight in dispersive ground; do not stop in the frontier borderlands.

Do not attack an enemy who occupies key ground first; in open ground, do not allow your formations to become separated and your communications to be blocked. In focal ground, ally with neighboring states; in serious ground, gather in plunder. In difficult ground, press on; in encircled ground, devise stratagems; in desperate ground, fight courageously.

In ancient times, those described as skilled in war made it impossible for the enemy to unite his front and his rear, for his divisions both large and small to cooperate, for his good troops to succor the poor, and for officers and men to support each other. When the enemy's forces were dispersed, they prevented him from assembling them; even when assembled, they threw him into disorder. They concentrated and moved when it was advantageous to do so; when not advantageous, they halted. Should one ask: "How do I cope with a well-ordered enemy host about to attack me?" I reply: "Seize something he cherishes and he will conform to your desires." Speed is the essence of war. Take advantage of the enemy's unpreparedness, make your way by unexpected routes, and attack him where he has taken no precautions.

The general principles applicable to an invading force are that when you have penetrated deeply into hostile territory your army is united and the defender cannot overcome you. Plunder fertile country to supply your army with plentiful provisions. Pay heed to nourishing the troops; do not unnecessarily fatigue them. Unite them in spirit; conserve their strength. Make unfathomable plans for the movements of the army. Throw the troops into a position from which there is no escape, and even when faced with death they will not flee. For if prepared to die, what can they not achieve? Then officers and men together put forth their utmost efforts. In a desperate situation, they fear nothing; when there is no way out, they stand firm. Deep in a hostile land they are bound together, and there, where there is no alternative, they will engage the enemy in hand-to-hand combat. Thus, such troops need no encouragement to be vigilant. Without extorting their support, the general obtains it; without inviting their affection, he gains it; without demanding their discipline, he wins it. Prohibit superstitious doubts and do away with rumors; then nobody will flee even facing death. My officers have no surplus of wealth, but it is not because they disdain riches; they have no expectation of long life, but it is not because they dislike longevity. On the day the army is ordered to set out, the tears of those seated soak their garments—the tears of those reclining course down their cheeks. But throw them into a situation where there is no escape and they will display the immortal courage of Zhuan Zhu and Cao Kuei. [Zhuan Zhu and Cao Kuei both lived in the Spring and Autumn Period, and were said to be brave warriors undaunted in the face of death.]

Now, the troops of those adept in war are used like the "simultaneously responding snake" of Mount Ch'ang. When struck on the head, its tail attacks; when struck on the tail, its head attacks; when struck in the center, both head and tail attack. Should one ask: "Can troops be made capable of such instantaneous coordination?" I reply: "They can." For, although the men of Wu and Yüe hate one another, if together in a boat tossed by the wind they would cooperate as the right hand does with the left. Thus, in order to prevent soldiers from fleeing, it is not sufficient to rely upon hobbled horses or buried chariot wheels. To achieve a uniform level of valor relies on a good military administration. And it is by proper use of the ground that both strong and weak forces are used to the best advantage. Thus, a skillful general conducts his army just as if he were leading a single man, willy-nilly, by the hand.

It is the business of a general to be serene and inscrutable, impartial, and self-controlled. He should be capable of keeping his officers and men in ignorance of his plans. He changes his methods and alters his plans so that people have no knowledge of what he aims at. He alters his campsites and marches by devious routes, and thus makes it impossible for others to anticipate his purpose. The business of a general is to kick away the ladder behind soldiers when they have climbed up a height. He leads the army deep into hostile territory and there releases the trigger. He burns his boats and smashes his cooking pots; he drives his men now in one direction, then in another, like a shepherd driving a flock of sheep, and no one knows where he is going. To assemble the army and throw it into a desperate position is the business of the general. To take different measures suited to the nine varieties of ground, to take aggressive or defensive tactics in accordance with different situations, and to understand soldiers' psychological states under different circumstances, are matters that must be studied carefully by a general.

Generally, when invading hostile territory, the deeper one penetrates, the more cohesion it brings; penetrating only a short way causes dispersion. Therefore, in dispersive ground, I would unify the determination of the army. In frontier ground, I would keep my forces closely linked. In key ground, I would hasten into the enemy's rear. In open ground, I would pay strict attention to my defenses. In focal ground, I would consolidate my alliances. In serious ground, I would ensure a continuous flow of provisions. In difficult ground, I would march past the roads speedily. In encircled ground, I would block the points of access and egress. In desperate ground, I would make it evident that there is no chance of survival. For it is the nature of soldiers to resist when surrounded, to fight to the death when there is no alternative, and when desperate to follow commands implicitly.

One ignorant of the plans of neighboring states cannot make alliances with them; if ignorant of the conditions of mountains, forests, dangerous defiles, swamps, and marshes, he cannot conduct the march of an army; if he fails to make use of native guides, he cannot gain the advantages of the ground. A general ignorant of even one of these nine varieties of ground is unfit to command the armies of a hegemonic king. Now, when a hegemonic king attacks a powerful state, he makes it impossible for the enemy to concentrate his troops. He overawes the enemy and prevents his allies from joining him.

It follows that there is no need to contend against powerful combinations, nor is there any need to foster the power of other states. He relies for the attainment of his aims on his ability to overawe his opponents. And so he can take the enemy's cities and overthrow the enemy's state. Bestow rewards without respect to customary practice; publish orders without respect to precedent. Thus, you may employ the entire army as you would one man. Set the troops to their tasks without imparting your designs; use them to gain advantage without revealing the dangers involved. Throw them into a perilous situation and they will survive; put them in desperate ground and they will live. For when the army is placed in such a situation, it can snatch victory from defeat. Now, the crux of military operations lies in the pretense of following the designs of the enemy; and once there is a loophole that can be used, concentrate your forces against the enemy. Thus, even marching from a distance of a thousand *li*, you can kill his general. This is called the ability to achieve one's aim in an artful and ingenious manner.

Therefore, when time comes to execute the plan to attack, you should close the passes, rescind the passports, have no further intercourse with the enemy's envoys, and exhort the temple council to execute the plans. When the enemy presents an opportunity, speedily take advantage of it. Seize the place which the enemy values without making an appointment for battle with him. In executing the plan, you should change according to the enemy situation in order to win victory. Therefore, at first you should pretend to be as shy as a maiden. When the enemy gives you an opening, be swift as a hare and he will be unable to withstand you.

# For Further Thought

Valued for its central location, Sun Tzu identifies the focal state as a key ally in maintaining diplomacy with others. Use the space below to draw parallels between the land of the focal state, and the various groups, departments, and organizations that you interact with. Who among them possesses the qualities of the focal state, making for a worthy ally?

# Chapter 12
# Attack By Fire

There are five ways of attacking with fire. The first is to burn soldiers; the second, to burn provisions; the third, to burn equipment; the fourth, to burn arsenals; and the fifth, to burn the lines of transportation. To use fire, some medium must be relied upon. Equipment for setting fires must always be at hand. There are suitable times and appropriate days on which to raise fires. "Times" means when the weather is scorching hot; "days" means when the moon is in Sagittarius, Alpharatz, *I,* or *Zhen* constellations, for these are days of rising winds.

Now, in fire attacks, one must respond to the changing situation.

When fire breaks out in the enemy's camp, immediately coordinate your action from without. But if the enemy troops remain calm, bide your time and do not attack at once. When the fire reaches its height, follow up if you can. If you cannot do so, wait. If you can raise fires outside the enemy camp, it is not necessary to wait until they are started inside. Set fires at suitable times. When fires are raised upwind, do not attack from downwind. When the wind blows during the day, it will die down at night. Now, the army must know the five different fire-attack situations and wait for appropriate times.

Those who use fire to assist their attacks can achieve good results; those who use inundations produce a powerful effect. Water can isolate an enemy, but cannot destroy his supplies or equipment as fire can.

Now, to win battles and take your objectives but to fail to consolidate these achievements is ominous and may be described as a waste of time. And, therefore, it is said that enlightened rulers must deliberate upon the plans to go to battle, and good generals carefully execute them. If not in the interests of the state, do not act. If you cannot succeed, do not use troops. If you are not in danger, do not fight a war. A sovereign cannot launch a war because he is enraged, nor can a general fight a war because he is resentful. For while an angered man may again be happy, and a resentful man again be pleased, a state that has perished cannot be restored, nor can the dead be brought back to life. Therefore, the enlightened ruler is prudent and the good general is warned against rash action. Thus, the state is kept secure and the army preserved.

# For Further Thought

Sun Tzu makes reference to the justification for battle. Reflect upon recent conflicts you have witnessed or engaged in, and determine whether the justifications were valid.

# Chapter 13
# Use of Spies

Now, when an army of one hundred thousand is raised and dispatched on a distant campaign, the expenses borne by the people together with disbursements of the treasury will amount to a thousand pieces of gold daily. In addition, there will be continuous commotion both at home and abroad, people will be exhausted by the corvée of transport, and the farm work of seven hundred thousand households will be disrupted. [In ancient times, eight families comprised a community. When one family sent a man to the army, the remaining seven contributed to its support. Thus, when an army of one hundred thousand was raised, those unable to attend fully to their own plowing and sowing amounted to seven hundred thousand households.]

Hostile armies confront each other for years in order to struggle for victory in a decisive battle; yet if one who begrudges rank, honors, and a few hundred pieces of gold remains ignorant of his enemy's situation, he is completely unaware of the interest of the state and the people. Such a man is no general, no good assistant to his sovereign, and such a sovereign no master of victory. Now, the reason a brilliant sovereign and a wise general conquer the enemy whenever they move and their achievements surpass those of ordinary men is their fore-knowledge of the enemy situation. This "fore-knowledge" cannot be elicited from spirits, nor from gods, nor by analogy with past events, nor by astrologic calculations. It must be obtained from men who know the enemy situation.

Now, there are five sorts of spies. These are native spies, internal spies, double spies, doomed spies, and surviving spies. When all these five types of spies are at work and their operations are clandestine, it is called the "divine manipulation of threads" and is the treasure of a sovereign. Native spies are those from the enemy's country people whom we employ. Internal spies are enemy officials whom we employ. Double spies are enemy spies whom we employ. Doomed spies are those of our own spies who are deliberately given false information and told to report it to the enemy. Surviving spies are those who return from the enemy camp to report information.

Of all those in the army close to the commander, none is more intimate than the spies; of all rewards, none more liberal than those given to spies; of all matters, none is more confidential than those relating to spy operations. He who is not sage and wise, humane and just, cannot use spies. And he who is not delicate and subtle cannot get the truth out of them.

Delicate, indeed! Truly delicate! There is no place where espionage is not possible. If plans relating to spy operations are prematurely divulged, the agent and all those to whom he spoke of them should be put to death.

Generally, in the case of armies you wish to strike, cities you wish to attack, and people you wish to assassinate, it is necessary to find out the names of the garrison commander, the aides-decamp, the ushers, gatekeepers, and bodyguards. You must instruct your spies to ascertain these matters in minute detail. It is essential to seek out enemy spies who have come to conduct espionage against you and to bribe them to serve you. Give them instructions and care for them. Thus, double spies are recruited and used. It is by means of the double spies that native and internal spies can be recruited and employed. And it is by this means that the doomed spies, armed with false information, can be sent to convey it to the enemy. It is by this means also that surviving spies can come back and give information as scheduled.

The sovereign must have full knowledge of the activities of the five sorts of spies. And the key is the skill to use the double spies. Therefore, it is mandatory that they be treated with the utmost liberality.

In old times, the rise of the Shang Dynasty was due to Yi Zhi, who had served under the Xia likewise, and the rise of the Zhou Dynasty was due to Lu Ya, who had served under the Yin. And, therefore, only the enlightened sovereign and the wise general who are able to use the most intelligent people as spies can achieve great results. Spy operations are essential in war; upon them the army relies to make its every move.

# For Further Thought

Sun Tzu's discussion of spying and espionage can be viewed through a modern perspective as a testament to the value of information. Reflect upon how significant pieces of key information have been invaluable in your past conflicts, and chronicle how the information was gathered, distributed, and used.

_____

_____

_____

_____

_____

_____

_____

_____

_____

_____

_____

_____

_____

_____

# The Hanzhang Interpretation
## Part I

# Chapter 1
# Strategic Considerations

The basic thesis of *Sun Tzu's Art of War* is to try to overcome the enemy by wisdom, not by force alone. Sun Tzu believed that a military struggle was not only a competition between military forces, but also a comprehensive conflict embracing politics, economics, military force, and diplomacy.

The attitude of Sun Tzu towards war is one of extreme prudence, earnestness, and seriousness. He said: "War is a matter of vital importance to the state; a matter of life or death; the road either to survival or to ruin. Hence, it is imperative that it be studied thoroughly."

# FIVE FUNDAMENTAL FACTORS
## OF WAR

Sun Tzu said: "One should appraise a war first of all in terms of five fundamental factors and make comparisons of various conditions of the antagonistic sides in order to assess the outcome. The first of the fundamental factors is politics; the second, weather; the third, terrain; the fourth, the commander; and the fifth, doctrine." In summary, Sun Tzu believed that one has to deliberate on the basic conditions which decide a war, and among them, five fundamental factors (*supra*) and seven elements (*infra*) are the primary ones.

In terms of politics, he meant that the sovereign should use political pressure or other means to bring the people into harmony with him. As for weather, he referred to the interaction of natural forces; the effects of day and night, rain and fair weather, cold and heat, time of day and seasons, and to make full use of favorable conditions and avoid any negative factors. By terrain, he meant distances, whether the ground is traversed with ease or difficulty, whether it is suitable for offensive or defensive tactics, and whether it is fit for the deployment of troops. As for the commander, he specified the general's qualities of wisdom, sincerity, benevolence, courage, tenacity, and strictness. By doctrine, he meant the discipline and organization of troops, the assignment of appropriate ranks to officers and their respective duties, regulations, and management of logistics.

These are the fundamental factors Sun Tzu believed to be imperative for analyzing and judging victory or defeat in a war. To analyze these factors, one has to answer the following questions, which were known as the "seven elements."

1. Which of the two sovereigns is more sagacious?

2. Which of the two commanders is wiser and more able?

3. Which of the two armies has the advantages of nature and the terrain?

4. On which side is discipline more rigorously enforced?

5. Which of the two armies is stronger?

6. Which side has the better trained officers and men?

7. Which side administers rewards and punishments in a more enlightened manner?

After making a comprehensive analysis, one will be able to forecast which of the two sides will be victorious. Of course, from the point of view of a modern war, these conditions are obviously insufficient. It was commendable, however, for Sun Tzu to discover these fundamental factors over two thousand years ago.

During China's war against Japan, Comrade Mao Zedong wrote a brilliant military essay, "On the Protracted War," in which, having analyzed the various factors of politics, economics, military affairs, diplomacy, and geography, he came to the conclusion that China would eventually be victorious over the Japanese invaders. History proved him to be right. China's enemy in a future war against aggression will be different from the Japanese, and the Chinese army will also be different. But Sun Tzu's ways of analyzing a war will remain practical and significant for China's war strategies.

## SUN TZU'S STRATEGIES OF WAR

Sun Tzu was extremely prudent as far as strategy was concerned. He considered it best to subdue the enemy's army without fighting. He pointed out: "To win one hundred victories in one hundred battles is not the acme of skill. To subdue the enemy without fighting is the supreme excellence." He reached this conclusion after carefully summing up the experience of past wars at that time.

Sun Tzu's principle of field operations was to take preemptive measures and seek quick decisions in campaigns. This principle was formulated from the historical and social conditions of that time. In his chapter entitled "Waging War," Sun Tzu said: "When the army engages in protracted campaigns, the resources of the state will not suffice. When your army is exhausted and its morale sinks and your treasure is spent, rulers of other states will take advantage of your distress and act. Then, even though you have wise counsellors, none will be able to make good plans for the future. Thus, though we have heard of excessive haste in war, we have not yet seen a clever operation that was prolonged." He again pointed out in the same chapter: "Those adept in waging war do not require a second levy of conscripts or more than two provisionings. They carry military equipment from the homeland, but rely on the enemy for provisions."

Why are quick decisions and preemptive measures required in a battle? This is determined by various social conditions, especially by the economic factors prevalent at the time of war. In Sun Tzu's time, a state was smaller than a province is today. Its population was small and materials limited. Thus, it was unable to support a protracted campaign.

## MARSHAL LIU BOCHENG'S TABOOS OF WAR

Marshal Liu Bocheng believed that one had to take into consideration the following five "taboos" in making strategic decisions:

**1.** Do not fight a war if the country is not powerful enough (including manpower and financial and military strength).

**2.** Do not fight a war if the situation is unfavorable (including the international situation and the attitudes of neighboring countries).

**3.** Do not fight a war if there is no domestic tranquillity.

**4.** Do not fight a war if the people do not support it.

**5.** Do not fight a war if the country has to fight on two or more fronts.

It is important to consider these five conditions in making a strategic decision, but they are not all required before a war is fought, nor are they of equal importance. The first and fifth conditions are more important than the others. Obviously, the victim of aggression should not be bound by those five taboos when it fights against the aggressor. And what is also obvious is that China should pay adequate attention to its defenses when it emphasizes economic construction while the international situation is still in turbulence and factors of war exist.

Marshal Liu also cited a number of examples to explain the five taboos: "It was stupid of General Tojo [of Japan] to unleash the Pacific War in 1941. While he was unable to pull one of his legs from the mire of China, he put the other leg into Southeast Asia, thus fighting on two fronts (against China and the United States, two big powers, on the one hand and the Southeast Asian countries on the other).

"Stalin was wiser. He had tried his best to come to terms with Japan while fighting against Nazi Germany. Meeting personally with the Japanese ambassador, he repeatedly expressed his wish to keep friendly relations with Japan and abide by the mutual nonaggression treaty between the Soviet Union and Japan. He declared war on Japan only when Germany had been defeated." There have been quite a few cases in which an army was defeated while fighting against more than one enemy; Hitler and Napoleon were only two of them.

It is always for a country's own fundamental interests and strategic posture that it make an alliance, conclude a treaty, or sign an agreement or convention with other countries after serious deliberations. After a treaty is concluded, unless it is an unequal one, it should be abided by within its period of validity; otherwise, the country or leader will lose credibility in the eyes of the world. Hitler was a man of such perfidiousness.

## *THE ART OF WAR* IN CHINESE HISTORY

Sun Tzu pointed out in *The Art of War*: "What is of supreme importance in war is to upset the enemy's strategic plans. Next best is to disrupt his alliances by diplomacy and the next best is to attack his army. The worst policy is to attack cities." This principle of Sun Tzu's is the quintessence of strategic ideas, which has been greatly valued by militarists in history, and is also a general rule to be observed in all anti-aggressive wars.

Sun Tzu did not elaborate upon his idea of upsetting the enemy's strategic plans. It is, therefore, necessary to give a few examples to explain what he meant. I think that Sun Tzu had a two-fold meaning: to make strategic decisions and to defeat the enemy with strategy. There have been numerous examples in China's history of war which can elaborate this principle.

*The Dialogue at Longzhong*

During the period of the Three Kingdoms (220–265 A.D.), Liu Bei went to the thatched cottage of Zhuge Liang three times, requesting assistance in Liu's struggle for domination of China. In *The Dialogue at Longzhong* (Shangyang County, Hubei Province), Zhuge put forward three principles which were typical strategic calculations:

**1. Advance westward and occupy Sichuan as a base, and then wait for the appropriate time to advance to the Central Plains (comprising the middle and lower reaches of the Yellow River).**

**2. Form an alliance with the kingdom of Wu in order that the forces of (Shu) Han will not be destroyed one by one.**

**3. Boycott Wei (Cao Cao) in the north, thus making the political situation clear to the people, winning them to Liu's side.**

Before Liu Bei asked Zhuge Liang to be his chief of staff, he had relied upon Yuan Shao to assist him. Liu Bei then went to Liu Biao for assistance without trying to have his own base. Why? This was because Liu Bei did not make a general analysis of the national situation and did not have a correct strategic decision. The Central Plains at that time were the scene of bitter struggles between various warlords. For this reason, there was hardly any possibility of Liu Bei establishing his own base there or setting up an army to fight against Cao Cao. Nor could he gain any advantage by making use of conflicts among warlords on the Central Plains.

Zhuge Liang made a thorough study in *The Dialogue at Longzhong* of the strategic position of Sichuan and came to the conclusion that Liu Bei must establish a reliable base there. Let us further analyze the three points in *The Dialogue at Longzhong*:

First, once it had Sichuan as a base, Liu Bei's army could recuperate and build up its energy before attacking the Central Plains. Sichuan, being rich in manpower and raw materials, had always been a land of abundance, and was, therefore, a reliable economic base for Liu Bei. Second, Liu Bei could avoid the danger of fighting on two fronts against Cao Cao as well as Sun Quan. Third, Liu Bei's army could take the initiative of advancing while carrying out an offensive and defending itself while retreating.

Liu Bei should make an alliance with the kingdom of Wu because at that time Wei in the north and Wu in the southeast were the only two powerful states left. To ally himself with Wu and boycott Wei would avoid fighting on two fronts and secure a peaceful environment in which to build up his strength. This policy made a clear distinction between enemies and friends.

Liu Bei should boycott Cao Cao because the power of the Han Dynasty then was, in fact, in the hands of Cao Cao, who in an attempt to put all of China under his rule gave orders to all the sovereigns in the name of the Emperor. It would be politically disadvantageous not to boycott Cao Cao. Liu Bei decided to revitalize the Han Dynasty in the name of being a close relative of the monarchy. His state of Sichuan was mountainous in the north, which was excellent for defense. Therefore, Cao Cao did not dare to attack Sichuan before he had conquered the kingdom of Wu in the east.

The purpose of expounding the strategy as Zhuge Liang stated in *The Dialogue of Longzhong* was to prove the importance of the idea of attacking an enemy's strategy.

### The Battle of Kuanlin

Another typical example of subduing the enemy by wisdom occurred in 354 B.C. The capital of Zhao at that time was Handan (in the present Hebei Province); the capital of Wei was Daliang (the present Keifan in Henan Province); and the capital of Qi was Linzi (the present Zibo in Shandong Province).

General Pang Juan of Wei directed an army of one hundred thousand men and surrounded Handan, the capital of Zhao. Zhao sent an emissary to Qi to ask for help. The sovereien of Qi summoned his generals and officials to discuss a plan to rescue Zhao. General Tien Ji offered himself as commander of a force of one hundred thousand men to fight against Pang Juan in order to rescue Zhao from the siege. But Qi's military adviser, Pang Bin, objected to it, saying that the best way of rescuing Zhao was to send an army to besiege Daliang, Wei's capital. He pointed out that the crack troops of Wei had all been sent to Handan, leaving its capital an unprotected city. When troops were sent towards Daliang, the sovereign of Wei would certainly order Pang Juan to come back and defend Daliang. The siege of Handan would be avoided without a fight. And when Pang Juan's troops were coming back to its aid, Qi's troops would choose a place to have a battle with Pang's troops to defeat them.

This stratagem was "to attack where he is sure to come to its rescue." It was a much better stratagem than General Tien Ji's plan to fight a battle with Pang Juan near Handan after a long and tiring march. Therefore, Qi's sovereign decided to send troops to Daliang under General Tien Ji's command with Sun Bin as his military adviser. When Qi's troops were on their way to Daliang, the sovereign of Wei, as expected, ordered Pang Juan to hurry back to Daliang with his army. The siege of Zhao was indeed ended without a fight. While the troops of Wei were retreating to Daliang, they came across Qi's troops at Kuanlin district, and were defeated. This was called the Battle of Kuanlin. In retrospect, we can conclude that Tien Ji's plan to help Zhao was one of attacking the enemy with strength, while Sun Bin's plan was to defeat the enemy with wisdom.

### The Battle of Ming Tiao

In 1763 B.C., Yi Ying defeated his enemy by strategic considerations after analyzing the situation and weighing the advantages and disadvantages. Yi Ying was one of Sun Tang's important officials, entitled Ah Heng—an official equivalent to a prime minister and chief of staff of the army. Yi Ying made suggestions that Sung Tang should refuse to pay tributes to Xia Jie in order to test his popularity and power over his people. Sung Tang accepted this suggestion and stopped paying tributes that year. Jie was furious and dispatched troops from nine tribes to attack Tang. Since Jie was still popular among his subjects, Yi Ying advised Tang to apologize to Jie and pay more tributes to him.

The second year Tang again refused to pay tributes. Jie was even more angry and wanted again to dispatch troops from the nine tribes to Tang. But this time the tribes were not so ready to send troops, complaining that they were poor. As a result of dispatching them every year, the soldiers were weary. Only three tribes answered the call and dispatched troops. Thereupon, Yi Ying said now that Jie had lost his popularity and fighting capacity and the morale of the troops sent by three tribes was low, this was the time to fight Jie. Sung Tang followed his advice and, together with the troops of other sovereigns, lay in ambush at Ming Tiao of Anyi (in the present Shansi Province) and defeated Xia Jie there. Then

Tang established the kingdom of Shang. Historically, this is known as the Battle of Ming Tiao. It is a typical example of finding an appropriate opportunity to defeat the enemy after analyzing the situation.

## DIPLOMACY

Sun Tzu attached great importance to diplomacy. He used to make alliances with forces in order to fight against a common enemy. The Wu kingdom at this time was situated at the place of the present Suzhou and Wusi. To its west was the powerful Cu kingdom (in present Hubei, Anhui, and Hunan provinces). They adjoined one another and had repeated border conflicts. Sun Tzu was eager to ally the Wu and Qi kingdoms in the north in order to alleviate pressure from that source and concentrate its forces in the fighting against Cu. The policy of disrupting an enemy's alliances in *Sun Tzu's Art of War* is a strategy of practical importance. This means to secure an advantageous posture strategically through diplomacy. It is also the idea of defeating the enemy by strategic considerations. The following three examples will suffice to elaborate this idea.

*Stalin's Nonaggression Pact with Hitler*

Before World War II, the Soviet Union tried its best to sign an agreement of mutual assistance with Britain and France in order to prevent the invasion of Nazi Germany. But the British and French rulers at that time attempted to direct the scourge of Germany towards the East—the Soviet Union. As a result, several talks between the three powers failed in spite of efforts made by the Soviet Union. Under the circumstances, Stalin could not have acted otherwise but to sign a nonaggression pact with Germany, which stopped the German advance for a certain period and thereby gave time for Soviet preparation. The British and French rulers were not as alert as the Soviet Union and suffered more immediately the force of Hitler's blitzkrieg. This was described by Comrade Mao Zedong as "to lift a stone just to crush one's own feet." Stalin's tactic of delaying the attack by Hitler through diplomatic means, thereby gaining time for preparation, was wise and desirable from a military strategic point of view.

### The Disruption of the Qi-Cu Alliance

During the Warring Period (475–221 B.C.), the kingdom of Qin wanted to attack Qi, but it feared the Qi-Cu alliance. Zhang Yi was, therefore, sent by Qin to Cu as an envoy to disrupt the Qi-Cu alliance. Upon arriving in Cu, Zhang Yi approached Queen Nan and presented her with a precious gift of pearls and jade and asked her to convey the following message to the sovereign of Cu: "Zhang Yi has been sent to Cu as an envoy to meet the sovereign of Cu. Qin is ready to cede six hundred *li* of its territory to the kingdom of Cu. What Qin asks for from Cu is only friendship and nonaggression."

The sovereign of Cu met with Zhang Yi, who tried all he

could to persuade Cu of the advantages of being on good terms with Qin. The sovereign of Cu was overwhelmed by its offer of territory (the equivalent of two hundred miles of land) as a reward for friendship and promised to be on good terms with Qin.

The sovereign of Qi was furious when he heard about the news of reconciliation between the sovereign of Cu and Zhang Yi, which he believed to be a conspiracy against Qi. After this, Qi and Cu became enemies.

In fact, the offer of two hundred miles of territory was a deception. When the envoy of Cu went to Qin to accept the territory, Zhang Yi said that what he had promised was not two hundred miles of Qin's territory but two miles of his own property. The Cu sovereign was extremely angry when he discovered this. He sent troops to attack Qin but was defeated. From then on, the kingdom of Cu became isolated from all sides. As a result, Qin's disruption of the Qi-Cu alliance laid the foundation for the defeat of Qi and Cu, respectively.

### The Alliance Between Jin and Qin

During the Spring and Autumn Period (770–476 B.C.), Zheng kingdom's disruption of the alliance between Jin and Qin kingdoms while being attacked by them was another convincing example of the use of diplomacy to weaken two allies. Zheng was a small state sandwiched between the two powerful neighboring states—Jin and Qin. Zheng, being allied with

Cu, hoped Cu would come to its rescue. Being afraid of Jin's and Qin's strength, Cu dared not to send any troops. Zheng was in a desperate situation.

Zheng's sovereign then sent his veteran official, Zhu Zhiwu—an experienced diplomat who was eloquent, courageous, and resourceful—to Qin to meet their sovereign in person. Zhu Zhiwu asked the sovereign of Qin for the reasons of its support to Jin in attacking Zheng. Qin's sovereign said he supported Jin because Zheng acted faithlessly towards Jin.

Zhu Zhiwu said: "Zheng did break its promise with Jin, but it has always highly admired and respected the great Qin. Your Excellency is wise and generous. You helped Jin in its establishment of the state. Now you are again helping Jin conquer Zheng by tiring your troops on a long expedition. Zheng is far away from Qin, and you would in no way be benefited if Zheng is conquered. On the contrary, if Zheng were occupied by Jin, it is Jin that would be greatly strengthened. And since Qin and Jin are adjoined to each other, if Jin becomes even more powerful, it will surely be a potential threat to Qin. I am worried for Qin's future. Jin is not a state that is unswervingly sincere and faithful. It promised once to cede its territory west of the Huang River to Qin, but it did not keep its promise. Moreover, it dispatched troops to the border to threaten the safety of Qin. Do you like to feed a close neighbor who is a tiger? In my opinion, the best thing for Qin to do is to withdraw from this expedition and come back. This is in Qin's interest. If Qin follows my advice and withdraws its troops, Zheng is willing to be Qin's protectorate, and, if necessary, provide military bases when Qin passes through the Central Plains. Zheng can also serve as a natural screen to protect Qin in the east and west against any threats from Jin."

The sovereign of Qin was left without any argument by this ingenious remark. A tacit understanding was then reached, and Qin withdrew its troops on its own. Seeing Qin's troops being withdrawn, and being aware that Cu was an ally of Zheng and that Cu would certainly come to its defense if Zheng were attacked, Jin also withdrew its troops immediately. The siege of Zheng was thus ended without a fight. This is one of the typical examples in China's war history in which a siege was avoided thanks to diplomacy only.

## WISDOM ON THE BATTLEFIELD

Regarding the principle of "the next best being to attack the army," it does not mean that one should try to defeat the enemy only by force. In fact, wisdom is extremely essential on any battlefield. There have been numerous examples of the need for strategic wisdom in China's history of war.

### The Battle of the Feishui River

In the year 383 B.C., General Fu Jian of the earlier Qin Dynasty led his army southward in an attempt to conquer East Jin. Xie Xuan and Xie Shi, who were Jin generals, ordered their armies to the southern bank of the Feishui River to resist Fu Jian, whose army (numbering more than three hundred thousand) was decidedly superior to that of Jin, which numbered only eighty thousand. Obviously, Xie Xuan and Xie Shi had to defeat their enemy with wisdom.

Xie Xuan's analysis of the two armies confronting each other across the Feishui River was that Fu Jian's army was superior in number, but its command was not unified. Infantry and cavalry were mixed and the vanguard and follow-up units were far apart. Moreover, the generals in Fu Jian's army had no strategic considerations. If its vanguard units were defeated, victory would be an easy task for East Jin.

Xie Xuan surmised that if he could attack the Qin army while it was in disorder, he would surely win. Then he sent an envoy to Qin, asking them to retreat for a certain distance so that the Jin army could cross the Feishui River and fight a decisive battle with Qin. The commander of the Qin army agreed and an order was given to retreat. There naturally was some disorder in the Qin army while it retreated, owing to its weak command.

Furthermore, Zhu Xu, a Jin officer who had surrendered to the Qin army, seized the opportunity to create disorder by shouting to the follow-up units, "The Qin army is defeated." The Qin soldiers in the rear were fooled by this ruse, and the infantry and cavalry vied in retreating. As a result, there was great confusion in the Qin army. The Jin army, after crossing the Feishui River, took advantage of this disorder, and swiftly attacked the Qin army and defeated it. Fu Jian, commander of the Qin army, was hit by an arrow, then fled alone to the north of the Hui River on horseback. This is known as the Battle of the Feishui River.

### The Battle of Gaixia

Another example of strategic wisdom in a war occurred in the year 202 B.C. The sovereign of Western Han asked Marshal Han Xin to direct the Battle of Gaixia against the Cu army, commanded by Xiang Yu, the sovereign of Western Cu. The Cu army was fairly powerful with a force of more than ninety thousand. In addition, Xiang Yu was valiant and courageous, and no one in the Han army dared to fight him alone. Pondering the problem carefully, Han Xin decided to devise a scheme. His army laid an ambush at the Jiulishan Mountain region. He asked Li Zuoche to enrage Xiang Yu and lure his army into the ambush. To make matters worse, Han Xin sent different units to fight against Xiang Yu in turn. The Cu soldiers could get neither food nor rest. Han Xin concentrated all his forces and fought a decisive battle against Cu.

During the battle, Xiang Yu was ambushed three times, and he had to lead the army personally more than a dozen times while attempting to escape, resulting in casualties of more than ten generals. In the end, Xiang Yu had to order a retreat because the soldiers were without food and reinforcements. Han Xin followed up his victory with a quick pursuit, not allowing Xiang Yu's men even a breathing spell. Xiang Yu committed suicide by cutting his throat. The remnants of the Cu army surrendered.

We can conclude that the Battle of Gaixia was won by Han Xin because of his correct strategy. If he had tried to win merely by force, it could have been a very different outcome, to say nothing of a complete annihilation of the Cu army.

## SUMMARY

Let us summarize what we have learned so far about Sun Tzu's theories relating to strategic considerations. At the very beginning of *Sun Tzu's Art of War,* he pointed out: "War is a matter of vital importance to the state; a matter of life or death; the road to survival or ruin. Hence, it is imperative that it be studied thoroughly." Therefore, one should appraise it in terms of the five fundamental factors and compare the seven elements. One has first to analyze and deliberate on the fighting capacity and advantages and disadvantages of one's own army and of the enemy. What is required of a commander is to "subdue the enemy troops without a fight" and to win by strategic considerations.

As we have seen, Sun Tzu advocated that in a war, generally the best policy is to attack the enemy's strategy. Next best is to disrupt his alliances by diplomacy. The next in order is to attack the enemy's army in the field, and the worst policy is to attack cities. His doctrine was that to fight a war is not only a matter of military affairs, but a matter relating to politics, economics, diplomacy, climate, and geography. Only when all these factors are taken into consideration comprehensively can one defeat the enemy. He was in favor of gaining the initiative by striking first, fighting a quick battle to force a quick decision, and not protracting a war. (These conclusions were reached according to the political and economic conditions in Sun Tzu's time.)

Sun Tzu believed that the state should make up the strategy of war, and the commander should organize and direct the battles. In other words, one should first devise a strategy in a safe command position that will ensure victory on whatever battlefield. All factors have to be considered practically and realistically without any wishful thinking.

Sun Tzu advocated that one should take the initiative and be flexible in fighting a war. Try to grasp the crux of the battle and attack where the enemy feels invulnerable, thus bringing about a decisive change. Then make the best use of the situation and guide the fighters to victory.

Devise a strategy in line with the fundamental and long-term interests of the state, not just expediency. It is much more complicated to devise a strategy than to lay a plan for a battle. One has to consider a much wider scope and take into consideration disadvantages as well as advantages, and try to develop and make use of all positive factors while reducing negative ones. (It is almost impossible to totally avoid the latter.)

Lastly, all things in the world have their strong and weak points, their advantages and disadvantages. They are dialectical and are transformed into their opposites under certain circumstances. But it is always the primary and key factor that is decisive, so one should never be misled by complicated minor factors.

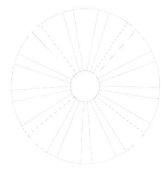

# Chapter 2
# Posture of Army

The chapter entitled "Posture of Army" in *Sun Tzu's Art of War* is a discussion of the way an army utilizes its position before a battle. By posture, Sun Tzu did not mean the formation or deployment of an army during a battle, but the strategically advantageous posture before a battle that enables it to have a flexible, mobile, and changeable position during a campaign.

In discussing "energy" or "posture," it would appear that Sun Tzu set out several necessary preliminary conditions for having the most advantageous position:

**1.** Those who are superior in military strength and weapons.

**2.** Occupation of a favorable terrain.

**3.** Excellent training of troops and high morale among soldiers.

**4.** Commanders who are resourceful, thoughtful, and good at seizing opportunities for combat.

A good posture is not inherent but comes from excellent art of directing war, rich experience in combat, and thoughtfulness in strategy and tactics on the part of the commanders. Sun Tzu pointed out:

"The energy of troops skillfully commanded in battle can be compared to the momentum of round boulders which roll down from a mountain thousands of feet in height. . . . When torrential water tosses boulders, it is because of its momentum; when a hawk strikes swiftly and breaks the body of its prey, it is because of timing. Thus, the momentum of a good commander is overwhelming and his attack precisely timed."

A brilliant commander seeks victory from the effect of combined energy and does not demand too much of his men. He selects his men and they exploit the situation. He should not only be skillful in employing various strategic considerations in order to change the disadvantages into advantages, he should also be good at creating momentum and regulating his troops, so that the attack can be both extremely swift and vigorous.

Generally speaking, those who are superior in military strength and weapons usually have an advantageous posture. But this is not universal. Sometimes one who is inferior can also be in an advantageous posture if he makes use of the situation and all the advantages that he has.

For instance, in southern China, there is a small animal, a kind of leopard, which is the same size as a cat. It is much weaker in strength than a tiger, but it often attacks a tiger when it sees one. It is as nimble as a squirrel and usually lays in ambush in a tree, and suddenly jumps onto the back of the tiger, gets hold of the tiger's tail, and uses its sharp paw to vigorously scratch the tiger's anus. The tiger jumps and roars from pain, but it is unable to reach the leopard cat. The only solution is for the tiger to roll on the ground, at which time the small animal flees rapidly.

The kingfisher is a small bird 15 centimeters long with green feathers and a sharp beak like a nail. It usually flies over water. When it sees a fish, it draws its wings in and dashes into the water with all its force like an arrow. Sometimes it can catch a fish bigger than itself. The action of a kingfisher fully illustrates what Sun Tzu stated: "the momentum is overwhelming and attack precisely timed."

## OPERATIONAL RESEARCH

In ancient Chinese history, there is a story about a horse race between the sovereign of Qi (Qi Wei Wang) and General Tien

Ji, in which Sun Bin assisted Tien Ji to win by exercising the concept of "operational research." Sun was aware of how his advice worked but ignorant of why.

Tien Ji often had horse races with the sovereign of Qi, but lost each time because Qi's horses were better. Qi's best horses ran 45 *li* per hour (equal to about 15 miles per hour), while Tien Ji's ran 43 *li;* Qi's next-best horses ran 41 *li,* Tien Ji's ran 40; Qi's worst horses ran 38 *li,* Tien Ji's ran 36 *li.* In each race, Tien Ji employed the same category of horses to race against the sovereign of Qi and lost in each. Upon learning this, Sun Bin suggested to Tien Ji that he first use his worst horses to race with Qi's best ones, a race he would no doubt lose. In the second race, Tien Ji should use his best horses to race with Qi's next-best ones, which would mean 43 *li* vs. 40 *li,* for a race he would surely win. In the third race, he would use his next-best horses against Qi's worst ones, 40 *li* vs. 38 *li,* and he would again win. Then Tien Ji would win two out of three races and be the overall winner.

Operational research has not yet been popularized in the sphere of war. It will be a science of how best to employ one's force when it is applied in the sphere of military science.

## THE ELEMENT OF SURPRISE

A commander who possesses wisdom and courage should try his best to have overwhelming momentum and take prompt action in a campaign. He should rely not only on his superior strength but also on all the advantageous factors so that he may be able to defeat his enemy with a surprise move.

There have been many examples in the history of the Chinese army during different periods of the Revolution when it was in an inferior position strategically, but was able to defeat the enemy by concentrating its forces on the offensive. It all depends on a commander's resourcefulness and flexibility to seize an opportunity in which he may be able to have overwhelming momentum and take prompt action. Battles fought by the First Field Army at Qinghua Bian, Yangmahe, and Yichuan in the 1940s were such examples. There are also many examples one can find in battles fought by other field armies. And most of them share the following common characteristics:

**1.** Flexibility in moving troops and skillfulness in seizing opportunities to fight.

**2.** Concentration of forces to defeat the enemies one by one.

**3.** Swiftness in moving troops and a comparatively short time spent in a battle.

**4.** Annihilation of enemies in one movement.

There are many factors which lead to advantageous posture for an army. For example, the terrain. In China, there is a saying: "With only one man guarding the mountain pass, ten thousand men are not able to pass." This does not mean that a single man can fight against ten thousand persons, but he who occupies an advantageous position can resist the attack of ten thousand men.

To take the enemy by surprise is another factor. In the East Han Dynasty, Emperor Guangwu attacked the rear of Wang Mang's army by surprise with his five thousand soldiers and defeated it. This is a typical case.

To gain initiative and be flexible is another important factor. For instance, strike first whenever possible and force the enemy into passivity. Attack promptly where the enemy is most vulnerable. Try to occupy a location of command that offers a good overall view of the battlefield.

Sun Tzu wrote in the chapter entitled "Maneuvering": "Close to the field of battle, they await an enemy coming from afar; at rest, they await an exhausted enemy; with well-fed troops, they await hungry ones. . . . Avoid the enemy when its spirit is keen and attack it when it is sluggish and the soldiers are homesick. . . . Do not engage an enemy advancing with well-ordered banners, nor one whose formations are in impressive array."

## SUMMARY

The following is a summary of Sun Tzu's thoughts regarding military posture:

Energy and favorable posture of an army come from the strategic considerations of commanders. A good commander must be deft at following Sun Tzu's principles: "Know the enemy and know yourself; in a hundred battles you will never be defeated." "Attack where the enemy is not guarded and catch him by surprise." "Defeat your enemy by a surprise move." "Attack the enemy at a place where the enemy is sure to come to its rescue."

A commander should try to move troops with overwhelming momentum and prompt action; he should have troops moving swiftly and fighting courageously.

A commander should have a correct understanding of a battle, and development of a campaign, and try to seize upon a favorable opportunity for fighting.

A commander should establish superiority of his army over the enemy's in number and in quality. (It is difficult to have an overall superiority, but to have partial advantages is possible.)

A commander should make use of advantageous terrains to make up for a lack of soldiers. Terrain can restrict the mobility of the enemy, which can even put it in a fatal position. However, if a good terrain is not properly made use of, the result will be catastrophic.

## Chapter 3
## Extraordinary and Normal Forces

Since the publication of *Sun Tzu's Art of War*, military scholars have devised many explanations of the "extraordinary and normal forces." In the book *Sun Tzu as Annotated by Eleven Scholars* (Sung Dynasty Edition), one of the annotators, Wei Liaozi, said: "The forces sent first to confront the enemy are normal ones, and sent later to attack the enemy are extraordinary ones." Cao Cao said something to the same effect.

In *A Dialogue Between Tang and Li*, Tang Taizong told Li Jing: "My normal forces would seem extraordinary to the enemy, and my extraordinary seem normal. That is exactly what is called deception. Extraordinary forces appear to be normal and normal, extraordinary; changes are unpredictable."

Li Jing also commented on the victory of the Battle of Huo Yi: "It would have been impossible for us to win, if normal forces had not been disguised as extraordinary and extraordinary, normal. Therefore, it all depends on the commander who decides how and when to use normal force or extraordinary."

Commenting on the subject, Marshal Liu Bocheng explained: "The normal forces and extraordinary forces are a dialectical unity, of which all generals must have a good grasp. Extraordinary forces contain normal ones, and normal, extraordinary. There should be unpredictable changes in them. . . . What are the normal forces? Generally speaking, forces which fight in a regular way according to usual tactical principles are normal forces. Forces which fight otherwise and move stealthily and attack the enemy by surprise are extraordinary ones."

Sun Tzu did not devote a separate chapter to the subject of the normal and extraordinary forces, but he included it in the chapter entitled "Posture of Army." For instance, he wrote: "There are unending changes of the normal and extraordinary forces. They end and recommence—cyclical, as are the movements of the sun and moon. They die away and are reborn—recurrent, as are the passing seasons. Generally, in battle, use the normal force to engage the enemy and the extraordinary to win. Therefore, the resources of those skilled in the use of extraordinary forces are as infinite as the heavens and earth, as inexhaustible as the flow of the great rivers. . . . It is the skillful operation of the extraordinary and the normal forces that make an army capable of sustaining the enemy's attack without suffering defeat."

It must be pointed out that Sun Tzu's use of the word "cyclical" seems to imply "cyclicalism." However, a careful study of the context would reveal that he used it as a metaphor to describe the changeability and unpredictability of employing extraordinary and normal forces. It is in no way related to cyclicalism and metaphysics, which denies the spiral development of all things.

## EXTRAORDINARY FORCES IN HISTORY

There have been numerous examples of battles in Chinese history in which victory has been achieved by catching the enemy by surprise.

### The Formation of Oxen With Fire

In the year 279 B.C., Qi's general, Tian Dan, was besieged in the city of Jimo. In order to save the kingdom of Qi, Tian Dan thought of a scheme. He collected more than a thousand oxen and covered each of them with a colorful cloth, then tied sharp daggers on their horns and dried reeds dipped in oil on their tails. He assembled five thousand soldiers all disguised as monsters. When night fell and the soldiers of the Yen army were all sound asleep, he lit the reeds on the oxen's tails. The oxen dashed towards the camps of the Yen army followed by Tian Dan's five thousand soldiers. The Yen army was caught by surprise and thrown into utter chaos. In this battle, Yen's troops were totally wiped out, and thereafter the victorious Tian Dan recaptured more than seventy cities in succession. The kingdom of Qi was saved from conquest. The battle was called the "Formation of Oxen with Fire" and has become a famous example of taking the enemy by surprise.

### The Campaign to Outflank Shu

In the year 263 A.D., in the late period of the Three Kingdoms, General Deng Ai of the kingdom of Wei was asked to attack the kingdom of Shu. Normally they had to attack Jianman Pass first. Knowing the pass was strongly fortified, Deng Ai directed his ten thousand troops to outflank the enemy. They marched along small paths in the Yingping Mountain Valley, crossing about two hundred miles of no man's land and even tunnelling through mountains. When they came to the perilous Mage Mountain, there was not even a path. He wrapped his body with a blanket and rolled down the mountain at the head of his men. Then his men came down one after another with the help of ropes, and quickly occupied Jiangyou Pass, and soon after, the city of Mianzu.

They advanced swiftly and reached Chengdu in November, taking the enemy by surprise. Liu Shan, general of Shu, was forced to surrender. This battle has been known for its suddenness and unexpectedness.

### The Battle of Guan Du

In the year 200 A.D., the troops of Cao Cao and Yuan Shao met in a confrontation at Guan Du. Yuan's troops were well provisioned and, therefore, able to withstand a protracted war, while Cao's troops ran short of provisions and could only fight a quick battle. Cao Cao was at his wit's end and very worried. Then, Xu You, one of Yuan's counsellors who committed crimes and feared prosecution, joined sides with Cao Cao, who was pleased to accept him.

At their meeting, Cao Cao said: "I want to defeat Yuan's army in a quick strike, but I think I am not able to do so because of the big gap in our strength. I am thinking of retreating but afraid of pursuit by Yuan's army. I hope you can give me counsel."

Xu asked Cao: "What do you think is the key problem in the battlefield?"

Cao said: "Yuan Shao can fight a protracted war because his provisions are abundant, while we cannot because of our poor provisions."

"So the key problem is provisions," said Xu. "Yuan's army stored their rations at Wucao, guarded only by a small force. You should raid Wucao and burn their provisions, which would surely result in chaos in Yuan's army."

Cao Cao followed his advice, raided Wucao, and burnt almost all of the provisions of Yuan's army. On learning about it, Yuan's troops were thrown into great confusion and soon retreated in disorder. Cao's troops pursued the chaotic Yuan army and defeated it. In this single battle, hundreds of thousands of Yuan's troops were destroyed. After that, Cao again defeated Yuan at Cang Ting.

Consequently, Yuan Shao died from a disease. His two sons fought for the throne and were both killed by Cao Cao. Since then, Cao consolidated his base in the northern area of the Central Plains and laid a solid foundation for the conquest of the whole Central Plains. As a result, the key to victory in a campaign sometimes does not lie in the battlefield but in devising apt strategies. This is another example of catching the enemy by surprise, which is called the scheme of "taking away the firewood from under the cauldron."

These are examples of employing extraordinary forces. Similar ones were numerous in the history of the People's Liberation Army (PLA). From them, we can say that Wei Liaozi's annotation might not be correct—that labelling a force normal or extraordinary has nothing to do with which occurs first. Deng Ai's extraordinary crossing of the Yingping Mountain Valley occurred before the real campaign started, as did the burning of Yuan's provisions by Cao Cao at Wucao.

The "Formation of Oxen with Fire" was arranged by Tian Dan to break the siege of the city of Jimo. Therefore, the extraordinary forces are used to take the enemy by surprise regardless of when they occur. We can safely say that Deng Ai did something normal contained in the extraordinary. Tian Dan's formation of oxen was something extraordinary contained in the normal.

During the Hui Hai campaign launched by the PLA in 1948, the fights between the Chinese military corps and the enemy troops were considered normal forces, but they also involved the use of extraordinary forces, such as Sun Tzu wrote: "to besiege a place to annihilate the enemy relief force," and "to make a feint to the east and attack in the west." Therefore, we say there were unending changes of the normal and extraordinary forces.

The extraordinary and normal forces are a dialectical unity and they are interchangeable. Normal forces can be turned into extraordinary ones in accordance with the changes in the field, and vice versa. Some of the commanders did not employ troops according to normal principles, such as "fighting with one's back to the river" or "cutting off all means of retreat," but they won.

The employment of troops should be subject to variations. The same military principle can be applied in different ways. In Chinese history, there have been a number of wars, some lasting hundreds of years (the Spring and Autumn

Warring Period), others lasting dozens of years (the anti-imperialist and anti-feudal wars in the contemporary period). The natures of these wars were obviously different; so were the ways of fighting. But many of Sun Tzu's principles and theories of war were applied in various ways in these conflicts. For instance: making correct estimates before engaging in battles; the deft application of strategic considerations; catching the enemy by surprise; taking the initiative; knowing the enemy and knowing yourself; concentrating large numbers of troops to fight a much smaller unit of the enemy. In short, as Sun Tzu pointed out: "Ingenuity in varying tactics depends on mother wit."

## SUMMARY

To summarize Sun Tzu's position on the use of extraordinary and normal forces:

Employment of troops must be extraordinary and varied so that the opponents cannot predict the movement of each other's armies. Sun Tzu said, "War is a matter of deception." That is to say, always attempt to throw your opponent into confusion.

Always try to catch the enemy by surprise. Use your troops at a place and time which are unexpected. Always try to strike a deadly blow at the enemy's weak point.

For the sake of extraordinary employment of troops, begin from a firm and unconquerable position. And then you should be farsighted, circumspect, courageous, and careful at the same time. Be able to move swiftly and to cope with any contingency.

Extraordinary and normal forces have interchangeable elements that resemble each other. This is dialectic in military affairs. You must avoid absolutes and not rigidly adhere to principles or articles in a military book. On the contrary, you should be flexible in applying them. Remember that there is no universal principle that leads to victory in every confrontation.

# Chapter 4
# Void and Actuality

In various chapters of *Sun Tzu's Art of War*, many important principles are given to guide the movement of an army. In the chapter entitled "Void and Actuality," Sun Tzu did not elaborate on this subject. Nevertheless, the major principles in it are immortal. For instance, he pointed out: "In making tactical dispositions, the acme is to leave no ascertainable shape. Then the most penetrating spies cannot pry, nor can the wisest enemy lay any successful plans against you. . . . Appear at places that the enemy must hasten to defend; move swiftly to places where you are least expected."

In the chapter entitled "Maneuvering," he wrote: "In war, practice deception and you will win victory. Move when it is advantageous to you. Concentrate or disperse your troops according to circumstances. When campaigning, move as swiftly as the wind; when marching, be leisurely, majestic and compact as the forest; in raiding and plundering, be like fire; in stationing, be firm as a mountain; when hidden, be unfathomable as the clouds; when striking, fall like a thunderbolt.

"Avoid the enemy when its spirit is keen, and attack him when it is sluggish and the soldiers are homesick. This is the art of controlling the moral factor. In good order, they await a disorderly enemy; in serenity, a clamorous one. This is the art of controlling the mental factor. Close to the field of battle, they await an enemy coming from afar; at rest, they await an exhausted enemy; with well-fed troops, they await hungry ones. This is the art of controlling the physical factor. They do not engage an enemy advancing with well-ordered banners, nor one whose formations are in impressive array. This is the art of changing with the circumstances."

In the chapter entitled "The Nine Varieties of Ground," he said: "Throw the soldiers into a perilous situation and they can survive; put them on death ground and they can live." In the chapter entitled "Estimates," he pointed out: "Attack the enemy where he is not prepared and where you are least expected." All these are important principles in war.

In ancient China, many books on the art of war discussed

the problem of void and actuality. Some compared them to yin and yang, meaning "void" is "yin" and therefore something false, and "actuality" is "yang," something true. This analogy is incorrect, or at least not precise. As a matter of fact, sometimes there is real action in "void," but most of the actions are deceptive. There are actions or movements which seem to begin from weakness, but they are to deceive and trap the enemy.

## VOID AND ACTUALITY IN WAR

Usually, there should be substance to any "void" movement so that you won't be defeated. It will amount to useless adventure if there is no solid backing. In military affairs, there are also constants (something solid or actual) and variables (void). Generally speaking, constants are dominant.

The following are a few examples of war to elaborate the application of "void and actuality."

### The Empty City Scheme

During the period of Three Kingdoms, the kingdom of Shu lost Jieting to Wei. Soon after, the Wei army, under the command of Sima Yi, advanced straight to the West City, which was an important place strategically, but not guarded because of Shu's lack of forces. Zhuge Liang knew he could not afford to lose the West City, which would have meant a total collapse of the Shu army. Being well aware that Sima Yi was suspicious and a coward, Zhuge Liang decided to create the illusion of an empty city, which scared Sima Yi and made him withdraw his army for thirteen miles. This action won time for Zhuge Liang so that he could await reinforcements.

The "Empty City Scheme" is not recorded in history books, but it appears in the notes of *The History of the Three Kingdoms*. Even if the story were not true, it would make sense. It tells us how to apply "void" and "actuality" in war. In this example, Zhuge Liang used the form of "void" to hint at the existence of his solid backing which he didn't have. He accomplished his purpose of scaring away Sima Yi's army. As a matter of fact, since he was not backed up by force, it was an adventurist policy.

### The Battle of Shijiazhuan

There is a similar more recent example of void and actuality in the history of the People's Liberation Army. In October 1948, Guomindang's General Hu Yi concentrated his 94th Army and three other divisions, including several thousand trucks, in an attempt to stage a quick raid at Shijiazhuan, which was then only guarded by two garrisons and training regiments of the PLA. Besides, there were three PLA regiments of the local army blocking Guomindang's advance north of Wuan County. Evidently it was not possible to stop the raid. Therefore, the commanders of the Jingcaji military area thought of a new variation of an "empty city scheme" and took the following measures.

First of all, the PLA spokesman of the military area declared on the radio that they were aware of and prepared for Guomindang's attempt to raid Shijiazhuan. He implied that if the army were to attack, they would not be able to retreat, which suggested the PLA's imaginary strength. Hu Yi listened carefully to the broadcast, then read it in writing. He had the same nature as Sima Yi—suspicious and cowardly. He became hesitant and asked his troops to advance carefully. Thus, the advance was slowed down.

Next, the commander of the military area ordered the local units to block the enemy's advance as far as possible north of Wuan County. He also ordered the defending troops of Shijiazhuan to build fortifications along the Futou River to show that they were well prepared for the attack. In the meantime, the commander ordered the army stationed below Changjiakou to move south to reinforce Shijiazhuan. And finally, the commander ordered the sixth column to wipe out the 49th Division sent by Yen Xishan to assist Hu Yi in raiding Shijiazhuan, thus cutting off the reinforcements for Hu Yi.

Several days later, Hu Yi was all the more restless, upset, and hesitant in regard to the direction he should take. He ordered his air force to carry out aerial reconnaissance missions over Shijiazhuan and discovered that the PLA was building fortifications along the Futou and Sha Rivers [in fact, they were false fortifications], and the city of Shijiazhuan was quiet.

Three days later, Hu Yi again ordered aerial reconnaissance missions and discovered that PLA troops were moving south near Yi County to reinforce Shijiazhuan, stretched as far as one hundred miles. He estimated them to number from eighty to one hundred thousand men from the crack troops of the PLA field army. Hu Yi calculated that this reinforcement would arrive before his army did. In the meantime, he learned of the destruction of the 49th Division sent by Yen Xishan. Finally, he ended the planned raid on Shijiazhuan and the city was saved.

For its defense, the PLA devised an "empty city scheme," which was weak, in fact, but apparently strong enough to slow down the enemy's advance. At the same time, they ordered troops to come down from the north to reinforce Shijiazhuan. Zhuge Liang's use of this scheme was adventurist, but the Battle of Shijiazhuan had solid backup. It was absolutely safe.

### The Battle of Malin Pass

In the year 341 B.C., the kingdom of Wei sent troops under the command of Pong Juan to attack Han. Han resisted with all its troops and fought five battles but was defeated. Han had to seek help from Qi. The sovereign of Qi sent troops to assist Han with Tian Ji in command and Sun Bin as chief of staff. Qi's troops advanced towards Ta Liang, Wei's capital, forcing Wei's army to withdraw from Han.

The sovereign of Wei sensed that Qi represented a serious threat to Wei, and there would be no peace for him if Qi were not defeated. He decided to concentrate all his crack troops with Pong Juan and Prince Shen as commanders to have a decisive battle with Qi.

Being aware of this, Qi decided not to fight Wei. Sun Bin advised Tian Ji: "Wei's troops are famous for their bravery and usually look down upon Qi. We should pretend to fear them. According to *Sun Tzu's Art of War,* in the forced march of one hundred *li,* the commander of the van will fall, and after fifty *li* only half the army will arrive." He suggested that Qi should withdraw its army in order to lure the enemy inside its territory, and at the same time, increase the number of soldiers while decreasing the number of cooking stoves. In other words, Qi should first pretend to be weak and then seize an appropriate moment to catch the enemy by surprise. Tian Ji accepted his proposal.

Wei's army pursued Qi's troops all the way, and Wei's scouts reported the first day that Qi had one hundred thousand cooking stoves; the second day, fifty; and the third day, only twenty. Pong Juan believed that there were a great number of deserters in Qi's army, so he ordered the Wei army to march with even quicker speed. He personally led several thousand soldiers and advanced day and night without rest. When they came to Malin Pass, they fell into the ambush of Qi's troops and were wiped out. Pong Juan himself was captured. Qi's troops then attacked Prince Shen's troops on the crest of their victory and captured him. Since then, Qi became the largest kingdom in the north. This is a typical example of adopting the form of "void" while being strong.

## SUMMARY

To summarize Sun Tzu's concept of void and actuality:

In employing troops, there must be interchangeable elements of "actuality" in "void," and "void" in "actuality." Normally, it is easier to adopt the form of "void" while being strong than from a weak position.

It is extremely important to know the characteristics of the enemy and its commander. It is also necessary to know the strong points of your various commanders so that you may ask them to do tasks for which they are best suited.

When you want to adopt the form of "void," do it reasonably, and there must be strength (solid backing) behind it (unlike Zhuge Liang's "empty city scheme"). You should take the initiative in your own hands, and adopt carefully worked out measures.

When you want to simulate an appearance, do it cleverly and reasonably so that the enemy is confused. Try to lure the enemy in deeply.

"Void" and "actuality" are interchangeable and limited by time. It is often difficult to see through the enemy's changes. Therefore, it is essential to have wise, active, flexible, courageous, and careful commanders.

# Chapter 5
# Initiative and Flexibility in War

Sun Tzu attached great importance to gaining the initiative in any confrontation. His principles of taking preemptive measures, of fighting a quick battle to force a quick decision, bringing the enemy to the battlefield instead of being brought there by him, are all for the sake of gaining the initiative in a war.

Mao Zedong said: "Losing the initiative means to be defeated, to be annihilated." Mao Zedong advocated that in fighting a battle you must bring the enemy where you want him to be, not run after him. He thought it better to gain mastery by striking only after the enemy has made the first move so that you may ascertain the enemy's weak points.

Initiative also means mobility and flexibility for the army. It means when it attacks, it is irresistible; when it defends, it is impregnable; and when it retreats, the enemy does not dare to pursue. There are many important statements to this effect in *Sun Tzu's Art of War*.

In the chapter entitled "Void and Actuality," Sun Tzu wrote: "An army may be compared to water, for water in its natural flowing avoids the heights and hastens downwards. So in a war, an army should avoid strength and strike at weakness. As water shapes its flow in accordance with the nature of the ground, an army manages to be victorious in relation to the enemy it is facing. As water retains no constant shape, so in war there are no constant conditions. One who can modify his tactics in accordance with the enemy's situation and succeed in gaining victory may be called divine."

In regard to "Maneuvering," he stated: "In war, practice deception and you will win victory. Move when it is advantageous to you. Concentrate or disperse your troops according to circumstances."

Writing about "Terrain," Sun Tzu said: "The general who is experienced in war once in motion is clear in his destination and never bewildered; once he acts, his resources are limitless and tactics varied. Therefore, I say: Know the enemy, know yourself, and your victory will never be endangered. Know the ground, know the weather, and your victory will be complete."

In referring to "Offensive Strategy," he wrote: "Know the enemy and know yourself, and in a hundred battles you will never be defeated. If you know only yourself, not the enemy, your chances of winning and losing are equal. If you are ignorant of either the enemy or yourself, you will surely be defeated in every battle."

The chapter entitled "The Nine Variables" pointed out: "A general who does not understand the advantages of the nine variable factors will not be able to use the terrain to his advantage, even though he is well acquainted with it. A general who directs troops and does not understand the tactics suitable to the nine variable situations will be unable to employ the troops effectively, even if he understands the 'five advantages.'" He emphasized in this chapter: "For this reason, a wise general in his deliberations always considers both favorable and unfavorable factors. By taking the favorable factors into account, he makes his plan and decision feasible; by taking into account the unfavorable, he may avoid disasters."

Sun Tzu's "The Nine Varieties of Ground" pointed out: "The skillful commander may be likened to *shuai-ran*, which is a kind of snake that is found in the Chang Mountains. When this snake is struck on the head, its tail attacks; when struck on the tail, its head attacks; and when struck in the center, both head and tail attack. . . . Therefore, exhibit the coyness of a maiden, until the enemy loses his alertness and gives you an opening, then move as swiftly as a hare, and the enemy will be unable to resist you."

While being aware of the disposition of an army, and of the extraordinary and normal forces, one must at the same time gain initiative and flexibility in employing troops. Sun Tzu wisely observed: "As water retains no constant shape, so in war there are no constant conditions." He meant there should be no fixed formulae for employing troops. One will surely be defeated by trying to apply one particular way of fighting to different situations or using a certain tactic derived from a specific instance for complicated battles. The way of staging a suitable campaign in a mountainous and forested area may not be applicable on the plains, and vice versa. Therefore, one should try to study and create new ways of fighting in accordance with the facts of each practical situation that presents itself.

The most important principle for directing a war is that there is no shortcut to master its laws. In a battlefield, events change quickly and often appear to be unpredictable. In fact, if one uses the theory of dialectical materialism in observing and analyzing the essence of war one will discover that (whether on the offensive or defensive, with strong forces or weak) there are always two sides to a question which are closely related and transform themselves into their opposites under certain conditions. Therefore, only when a commander engages in a war can he gain insight into the objective factors that promote this transformation of opposites, and avoid disadvantages and make correct decisions leading to victory.

## DEFTNESS, FIERCENESS, AND SWIFTNESS IN WAR

In this respect, Marshal Liu Bocheng stresses deftness, fierceness, and swiftness. He said: "Flexibility in employing troops is reflected by taking measures of void or actuality deftly, such as making a feint to the east and attacking in the west, changes in the extraordinary and normal forces, diverting the enemy as you wish and making him take what you want to give, and attacking where the enemy is sure to come to the rescue and where it is most unexpected."

### The Battle of the Cheshui River

One of Mao Zedong's most valuable attributes was his initiative and flexibility in directing a war. He often defeated his enemy by a surprise move. The Battle of the Cheshui River during the Long March was a typical example.

The Cheshui River winds through the borders of Yunnan, Guizhou, and Sichuan Provinces. In January 1935, Mao Zedong decided that the Red Army should march northward from Zunyi (by way of Tongzi, Songkan, and Tucheng) and then cross the Cheshui River. The enemy was very worried about this movement. The pursuing Central Army and the provincial troops of Sichuan, Guizhou, and Hunan quickly concentrated in that area, trying to encircle the Red Army.

Aware that it was now impossible to cross the Yangzi River, Mao Zedong ordered the Red Army to assemble in that area and await new opportunities. When he found out that the enemy in Guizhou Province was weak, he ordered the army to advance suddenly eastward, crossing the Cheshui River again, and went back to attack Tongzi and Zunyi (both in Guizhou Province) again. During the march, the Red Army annihilated twenty regiments of the enemy. Jiang Jieshi was extremely dismayed by the defeat and moved troops again in a new attempt to besiege the Red Army in the Zunyi Area.

In order to confuse and then move the enemy troops, Mao Zedong ordered the Red Army to march through Renhui and cross the Cheshui River for the third time at Maotai; then he advanced northward to southern Sichuan. Seeing this movement, Jiang Jieshi believed that the Red Army would cross the Yangzi River again and join forces with the Fourth Front Army. So he ordered the provincial troops of Sichuan, Guizhou, and Hunan and the Central Army to encircle the Red Army again in an attempt to wipe them out in a single strike.

Judging that the enemy was being moved according to his plan, Mao Zedong directed the Red Army to suddenly turn east, crossing the Cheshui River for the fourth time, and, in a rapid march along the right wing of the enemy troops, crossed the Wujiang River and marched towards Guiyang (the capital of Guizhou). While the main force of the Red Army feigned an attack on the capital, other troops broke through the area between Guiyang and Lungli, crossing the Hunan-Guizhou Highway, advancing towards Kuanming (the capital of Yunnan Province).

Discovering that they had been taken in, the enemy marched over 300 miles to come back to defend Kuanming. By this time, the Red Army had already crossed the Jingsa River with seven small boats in nine days and nights, reaching Huili in Sichuan. Thus, the Red Army had extricated itself from the pursuit and encirclement tactics of the Guomindang troops and realized its strategic aim of crossing the Yangzi River and going to the north of China.

From the above example, we can see Mao Zedong's masterful use of flexible tactics and excellent art of war. He directed the operations of the Red Army with miraculous skill, often beyond the expectations of the enemy. The Red Army advanced in great strides, puzzling and directing the enemy, making them weary and finally succeeding in freeing itself from their pursuit.

Mao Zedong's example illustrates the importance of selecting proper generals. An inadequate commander may succeed in one action but may well lose the overall situation. It is because he cannot adapt himself to radical changes in the field and, therefore, is unable to put into effect his superior's strategic intention. For example, during the period of the

Three Kingdoms, Zhuge Liang could well be called an effective chief of staff who was good at tactical planning, but he made a mistake in assigning Ma Su as a general for the defense of Jie Ting. Ma Su had some military knowledge; however, he lacked the ability to take charge of the overall situation, and did not have the experience of employing troops flexibly. He was, in fact, a pedant.

### The Battle of Jingzhou

During the period of the Three Kingdoms, Jingzhou was occupied by the kingdom of Shu and was garrisoned by the famous general Guan Yu. The kingdom of Wu had tried to reclaim its possession of Jingzhou but had been unsuccessful. In 219 A.D., the sovereign of Wu, following General Lu Meng's advice, made an agreement with Cao Cao to attack Jingzhou from the north and south simultaneously (Cao's army from the north to be led by General Cao Ren; Wu's army from the south to be led by Lu Sun).

At first, Lu Sun's army was led by Lu Meng, who was well known for his resourcefulness and bravery. Guan Yu was most cautious regarding him. Lu Meng thought of a scheme of luring the enemy away from its base. He pretended to go back to Jianye because of illness and recommended that Lu Sun take his place. When Guan Yu heard the news, he was relieved. Thinking that Lu Sun was a young general who had not much fighting experience, Guan Yu attacked Shangyang and

Fancheng in the north with crack troops led by him personally, leaving Mi Fang and Fu Shireng to guard Jingzhou.

When Lu Meng learned all this, he knew his scheme was successful. He ordered several hundred men disguised as merchants to go to the northern boundary between the kingdoms of Zhu and Wu and strike at the fortresses along the river with many troops, forcing Mi Fang and his men to surrender.

However, the northward advance of Guan Yu's troops progressed smoothly. They captured Xiangyang and threatened the city of Fancheng. Yu Jing and Pang De, Cao Cao's senior generals, were both captured, and large numbers of their troops were annihilated. Cao Cao was panic-stricken and began to think about moving his capital.

Guan Yu was bitterly remorseful when he learned that Jingzhou had been attacked and taken by the Wu army. He immediately withdrew his troops and retreated towards Maicheng where he was besieged by the Wu army. Guan Yu fell into an ambush and was captured.

Lu Meng's scheme of luring the enemy away from its base was successful because he knew Guan Yu was arrogant and had a fondness for the grandiose. Lu Meng asked Lu Sun to take his place in order to completely disarm Guan Yu psychologically. The way Guan Yu led all his troops northward was a manifestation of his desire for honor. It is extremely important for a commander to know the characteristics of his opponents' generals and try every means to win the battle with strategy.

*The Liaoxi-Shenyang Campaign*

During the Chinese War of Liberation [1945–49], the tactical situation in the northeastern battlefield under Lin Biao was unfavorable as a whole to the PLA. He had besieged Changchun and crossed the Songhua Jiang River three times, but had not gained the initiative or flexibility in the campaign. Lin Biao's forces were superior to Wei Lihuang's, the Guomindang general. However, in the opinion of the PLA's Mao Zedong and Zhou Enlai, this was because of errors made by the PLA commander in that region.

After deep deliberation, Mao Zedong and Zhou Enlai decided to attack Jingzhou, which was considered a strategic move whereby the enemy would be obliged to defend a valuable position. Jingzhou was the key junction for the passage of supplies between northern and northeastern China. If Jingzhou were taken, supplies for the Guomindang army in the northeast region would be cut off. Moreover, the mutual strategic support of the enemy forces in the northern and northeastern regions would also be lost. If Jingzhou were attacked by the PLA, the enemy would have to come to its rescue in a strategically weak position by the PLA's initiative. If reinforcements were to be sent, the Guomindang army would run the risk of being wiped out while they were in motion, thus creating the conditions for the PLA to move troops flexibly.

History proved the correctness of the decision made by Mao Zedong and Zhou Enlai. Just as expected, when

Jingzhou was being attacked by the PLA, reinforcements were sent from northern China by the enemy, but were intercepted by the PLA and failed to reach Jingzhou. The Guomindang troops were also dispatched from Shenyang to rescue Jingzhou and were intercepted and annihilated at Dahushan. Later, the enemy in Changchun had to surrender. In this campaign, a total of more than 470,000 Guomindang troops were wiped out. The whole of the northeastern region was liberated.

It can be concluded that strategic initiative is not innate in a battle, but has to be created by wise commanders. Flexibility of tactics in a campaign is generally obtained on the basis of strategic initiative. The Liaoxi-Shenyang campaign illustrates the truth of this theory.

## SUMMARY

Grasp the key point which affects the whole campaign: Deftness, fierceness, and swiftness should be understood correctly. Deftness means that a plan is put into execution craftily; fierceness is an overwhelming superiority of force, as a fierce tiger springs upon a goat; swiftness means that a battle is ended as suddenly as a flash of lightning.

Initiative and flexibility require that feints and strikes be varied, moves of the enemy be planned and directed. Attack where the enemy will surely come to its own rescue, and have several feasible alternatives in hand before starting a campaign.

Initiative in a campaign is not innate but has to be fought for. It largely depends upon the commander's ability to direct a battle in accordance with the change of events. One can change an unfavorable situation into a favorable one and passivity into initiative (*e.g.,* the four-time crossing of the Cheshui River and the Battle of Jingzhou). Those who employ troops flexibly usually will have the initiative.

Choose a suitable commander who has creativity of thought and the ability to react speedily. There is neither a set form of employing troops nor an overall rule for winning a war. One has to blaze new trails constantly.

Attach importance to the creation of a brain trust, which knows how to train staff officers as thinkers. They should not be used as copy clerks or orderlies. This is the only way in which a commander can pool the wisdom of his staff.

# Chapter 6
# Use of Spies

"Use of Spies" is the title of the last chapter of Sun Tzu's Art of War. It points out the importance and the ways of using spies in a battle. The purpose of their use is to be aware of one's enemy. This develops Sun Tzu's idea: "Knowing the enemy and oneself, one will be invincible." Let us see how Sun Tzu explored this topic.

In the chapter on spies, Sun Tzu wrote: "The reason the enlightened sovereign and the wise general often win the battle when they move, and their achievements surpass those of ordinary men, is foreknowledge. This foreknowledge cannot be elicited from spirits or gods, nor by analogy with experience, nor by astrologic calculations. It must be obtained from men who know the enemy's situation.

"In olden times, the rise of the Shang Dynasty was due to Yi Zhi, who had served under the Xia. The rise of the Zhou Dynasty was due to Lu Ya, who had served under the Yin. Therefore, only the enlightened sovereign and wise general who can use the most intelligent people as spies can achieve great results.

"Now there are five sorts of spies: native spies, internal spies, double spies, doomed spies, and surviving spies. When all these five types of spies are at work and their operations are clandestine, it is called the divine manipulation of threads and is the treasure of a sovereign.

"The sovereign must understand the activities of all five types of spies. He depends mainly on double spies for knowledge of the enemy situation, and therefore it is mandatory that they be treated with the utmost liberality. Hence, of all those in the army close to the commander, none is more intimate than the spies; of all rewards, none more liberal than those given to spies; of all matters, none is more confidential than those relating to spy operations."

The most valuable aspect about *Sun Tzu's Art of War* is that he worked out his strategies and tactics from actual war conditions and on the basis of full knowledge of the enemies. His idea of obtaining intelligence or attaching importance to men who know the enemies' situation is material. He used various means to collect information on an extensive scale. He was resolutely against the belief in spirits or gods, analogy with past events, and astrologic calculations applied to war strategies.

Sun Tzu wrote: "Native spies are those from the enemy's country people whom we employ. Internal spies are enemy officials whom we employ. Double spies are enemy spies whom we employ. Doomed spies are those of our own spies who are deliberately given false information and told to report it to the enemy. Surviving spies are those who return from the enemy camp to report information." Indeed, when these five types of spies are all at work, there is no respite for the enemy.

As for the scope of collecting information, Sun Tzu pointed out: "In the case of armies you wish to strike, cities you wish to attack, and people you wish to assassinate, it is necessary to find out the names of the garrison officers, the aides-de-camp, the ushers, gatekeepers, and the bodyguards. Our spies must be instructed to ascertain these matters." It goes without saying that the size of an enemy's areas and the population and the storage of his materials are all within the scope of espionage.

## THE HISTORY OF SPIES

Those who have studied the history of Chinese and foreign wars are aware that the use of spies has been an important means of fighting a war. No doubt, the ways of espionage have developed from primitive to complicated. Despite the highly technical age that we live in, which enables us to use all modern devices including satellites, the use of spies still remains worthwhile for intelligence gathering between countries. The basic form of spying does not differ that much from what Sun Tzu summed up more than two thousand years ago. The following are examples of using native spies in ancient as well as modern times.

### The War Between Chu and Han

During the war between the kingdoms of Chu and Han, an important official of the Chu army named Fan Zhen was well known for his resourcefulness and respected by Xiang Yu, the sovereign of Chu. Zhang Liang and Chen Ping, both counsellors in the court of Han, feared Fan Zhen because of his ability to see through schemes.

Chen Ping knew that Xiang Yu was very suspicious, so he thought of an excellent plan to use in their war. He sent a messenger with gifts and a fabricated letter to Fan Zhen to impersonate Fan Shi, Fan Zhen's nephew. In the letter, Fan Shi wrote that he was now an adviser under Liu Bong, the sovereign of Han. He said Liu Bong was an open-minded and magnanimous ruler, so he was extremely happy serving him. The messenger specifically went to the Chu camp at a time when Fan Zhen was not there. He gave the letter and gifts to the sentry who thought it important to forward directly to Xiang Yu. Xiang Yu became suspicious after reading the letter. When Fan Zhen came back, Xiang asked him whether he had a nephew named Fan Shi. Fan Zhen confirmed this but added that Fan Shi had died in his boyhood. Xiang Yu was then all the more suspicious that Fan Zhen had colluded with Liu Bong.

The next year, the representatives of Liu Bong and Xiang Yu started peace talks. When Xiang Yu's representative arrived in Han, Chen Ping pretended that he was expecting a representative from Fan Zhen rather than Xiang Yu. He had cancelled the rich feast which was supposed to have been given in honor of Fan Zhen's man. Instead, Chen Ping served Xiang Yu's representative with an ordinary dinner. When Xiang Yu heard about what happened in Han, his suspicions about Fan Zhen increased. Then he never listened to Fan's advice again. The relationship between them became strained day by day. Fan Zhen was forced to resign, and he died on his way back to his hometown. Until his last day he was unaware as to the reason for Xiang Yu's change of attitude towards him. After that, Xiang Yu made all decisions on his own and courted defeat in the end. Chen Ping's scheme of driving a wedge between Xiang Yu and Fan Zhen succeeded.

During the period of the Three Kingdoms, Zhou Yu of the kingdom of Wu used the same kind of scheme which prompted Cao Cao to kill Cai Mao and Chang Yong, both of whom were his own admirals. As a result of this, Cao Cao was defeated in the Battle of Chibi.

*Hitler's Fabrication of Soviet Spies*

On the eve of World War II, Hitler's intelligence officers fabricated information framing a case against General Tuhachevski, who was then a senior officer in the Soviet Red Army's Supreme Command. The information falsely accused him of working with Germany in an attempt to overthrow Stalin's leadership by force. A Soviet spy in Germany bought the information for a hundred thousand roubles. The Soviet Supreme Command was taken in, and not only was Tuhachevski shot, but a number of other Soviet generals were also implicated. This was one of the factors which accounted for the failure of the Soviet army in the beginning of the war against Nazi Germany.

## SUMMARY

Native and double spies are the most important types of spies to use against an enemy. Properly used, they can jeopardize the enemy's unity and disintegrate his forces. An enemy can also be disarmed by its own hand being caused to engage in internal strife.

Use of spies must be kept highly confidential. They must be extremely alert and resourceful; otherwise they are apt to be cheated, especially by double spies.

Spies must be liberally rewarded and their work highly appreciated. Spies must be boldly used. Their scope of activity and occupation must not be restricted. The only thing demanded of a spy is to fulfill the task for which he is entrusted.

# Chapter 7
# Geography

Of the thirteen chapters in *Sun Tzu's Art of War*, four chapters—"The Nine Variables," "Marches," "Terrain," and "The Nine Varieties of Ground"—deal with the relationships between geography and military affairs. In other chapters, there are also passages relating to geography.

## THE IMPORTANCE OF TERRAIN
The "Terrain" chapter pointed out: "Conformation of the ground is of great assistance in battle. Therefore, to estimate the enemy's attempts and to calculate the degree of difficulty

and distances of the terrain in order to control forces of victory are tasks of a superior general. He who fights with full knowledge of these factors is certain to win, and he who does not is sure to be defeated."

It must be made clear that what Sun Tzu meant by terrain is not the same as a modern definition. It is rather a concept which has the implications of the modern "topography" and "military geography."

Although Sun Tzu thought conformation of ground an assistance in battle, he asserted that a senior commander must be fully aware of the degree of difficulty and distances of terrain. Facts have proven his assertion. There have been numerous examples, abroad as well as in China, in which an army was defeated because of ignorance of terrain.

For example, in the year 645 B.C., the kingdoms of Qin and Jin fought at Han Yuan (in present Shanxi Province). The war chariots of Jin got stuck in the mire because the Jin commanders were ignorant of the terrain there. As a result, the Jin army was not only defeated, but Jinhuigong, the commander, was also captured.

In the year 589 B.C., Qi kingdom was defeated by Jin. In retreating, its chariots were entangled in a big clump of trees, almost resulting in the capture of its sovereign.

Sun Tzu, summing up numerous examples of this kind, explained some of the effects that geography has on war. In the chapter entitled "Terrain," he classified it in six types:

"accessible," "entangling," "temporizing," "narrow passes," "precipitous," and "distant." These types are terrains that are natural to a battlefield, and which fall generally into the category of topography.

In the chapter entitled "Nine Varieties of Ground," he categorized ground as "dispersive," "frontier," "key," "open," "focal," "serious," "difficult," "encircled," and "desperate." These anticipated geographical situations, which include strategic places beyond a boundary, are generally related to military geography.

In his book, Sun Tzu discussed each category in detail and the ways to handle them. He gave much emphasis to fighting in a marsh or in a covered place. He pointed out: "In crossing marshes, do it speedily. Do not linger in them. When on march you find dangerous defiles or ponds covered with aquatic grasses, or hollow basins filled with reeds, or woods with dense tangled undergrowth, search them out carefully, for these are places where ambushes are laid and spies are hidden."

This principle is still applicable in modern wars. In World War I, one hundred thousand Russian troops led by General Shamansonov were completely annihilated by the German army in a marsh. And one can cite a number of examples in the modern history of war in which troops were intercepted and defeated at dangerous defiles and covered places.

# FOCAL GROUND

The importance of focal ground in connection with the strategic deployments developed by the United States and the Soviet Union [during the latter half of the twentieth century] —is obvious and will be considered here.

Sun Tzu's definition of focal ground is: "The area which is at the junction of three states is focal. He who gets control of it will gain the support of surrounding states. . . . On focal ground, make allies of those states. . . . And I should consolidate my alliances."

Focal ground, generally speaking, is outside one's own territory, but it is strategically most important. If one occupies it first, one will be in a most favorable position. Apparently, since the focal ground is outside one's boundary, it can be far away. It is not easy to get control of it by mobilizing one's troops. Therefore, Sun Tzu's means of taking control was to make allies of the states neighboring the focal ground, which seems to be reasonable and feasible.

In the book *Sun Tzu's Art of War as Annotated by Eleven Authors* (Sung Edition), eight of the writers had the same explanation with regard to focal ground. They all believed that it is a strategically important place which has roads extended in all directions. It is vital, therefore, to have it under control first. The means to obtain it is, however, not by force but by diplomacy.

The following comment by Mr. He is representative of the opinions of others: "Focal ground is a junction which extends in all directions. Take hold of it first and the others will obey you. It gives security to get but is dangerous to lose.

"The sovereign of Wu once asked Sun Tzu: 'If we are far off from the focal ground, we won't be able to reach it first even if we drive our horses and chariots as fast as possible. What shall I do?'

"Sun Tzu replied: 'The distance is the same to us and to the enemy. To get control of the focal ground, we must attach more importance to wealth than force. If you reward your prospective allies with valuables and bind them with solemn covenants, you are there first even if your troops have not arrived. You are aided and your enemy is not.'"

The meaning of his comments is clear. The main idea is to adopt diplomatic measures and economic means to win over the state in which the focal ground is situated.

## THE RIVALRY BETWEEN THE U.S. AND U.S.S.R.

Sun Tzu's theory in this respect is of practical significance, which can be proven by examples of rivalry between the United States and the Soviet Union. Karl von Clausewitz often proved the correctness of his theoretical conclusions by giving examples from war history. He also attached great importance to topography and once said that it is of special significance for the headquarters of the general staff to have knowledge of geography. And one can always find records of terrain in war history. Therefore, each headquarters of the general staff presently in various countries has set up a specific department to study geography.

According to the definition Sun Tzu gave to focal ground and the annotations on it, there are quite a few strategically important places which can be said to be focal ground: the Strait of Gibraltar, the Suez Canal, and the Strait of Bosphorus—the three passages in the Mediterranean Sea and the southern wing of NATO; the Strait of Malacca, between Indonesia and Malaysia; the Panama Canal in Central America; and the Persian Gulf and Gulf of Mexico—one in the East and one in the West.

As is known, one of the superpowers found it difficult to lay its hands on the Strait of Gibraltar, which was firmly in the hands of the United Kingdom. But it spent several billion dollars as military and economic "aid" to Egypt in order to get the right of passage through the Suez Canal; it gave one billion dollars as "aid" to Turkey, and its principal leader visited the country personally to ensure its right of passage through the Strait of Bosphorus, which it succeeded in obtaining. The aircraft carrier *S.S. Kiev* secured a smooth passage through the Strait of Bosphorus into the Mediterranean, which was not permitted according to an international treaty. What this superpower did was in line with Sun Tzu's principle: "One should attach enough importance to giving aid and send more envoys. . . ."

The United States and the Soviet Union fought for control of Afghanistan and several other countries around the Persian Gulf. The policy of Cuba, the focal ground east of the Gulf of Mexico, greatly changed the strategic positions of the two superpowers in North and South America.

Tonga, a small country in the South Pacific, is at the strategic point among three allies: the United States, Australia, and New Zealand. The Soviet Union once tried to cater to this country by "giving economic aid and sending a number of envoys" in an attempt to get a foothold in the South Pacific. It did not succeed because its scheme was seen through.

## GEOGRAPHY IN THE SPACE AGE

The world has entered the space age, and various kinds of satellites have been widely used for military purposes, especially the space shuttle. All this has made it possible for a future war to be fought in space. But nothing can completely escape the confines of earth. Satellites and space shuttles alike are both launched from the ground, where the strategic points and economic bases are also located.

Therefore, geography is one of the four indispensable factors—in addition to the enemy's and one's own situations and the element of time—to be taken into consideration before making decisions and laying out plans. No doubt, this is taught in all military academies in the world. When we study *Sun Tzu's Art of War,* we should in no way neglect the practical significance of his doctrine with regard to geography.

## SUMMARY

Places of strategic importance include straits, canals, airports, gulfs or bays, and launching sites for guided missiles which are worthy of blockade and control. There are generally two ways of controlling them before the enemy does: One is to make an ally through diplomacy of the country where the place is situated; the other is to rent or lease the place through friendly negotiations so that it may not be used by the enemy.

Deserts, big marshes, forests, uninhabited areas, plagued regions, and high mountains where the air is thin are unfit places for a military troop to inhabit for long.

There are places one must fight for militarily. They include centers of communication or of military, political, or economic importance. It is advantageous to occupy places where one can be the master of the situation, preserving the freedom to move troops. Places from which one can attack as well as retreat, where one can keep plentiful supplies, and where one can adapt to all kinds of changes are all important.

Tactically valuable places generally are commanding heights above a battlefield, hubs of communication, solid and strong buildings on flatlands, bridgeheads, and certain places for crossing along a river.

The Hanzhang Interpretation
# Part II

# Chapter 8
# Historical Background of
# Sun Tzu's Art of War

Mao Zedong wrote in an article: "Where do correct ideas come from? Do they drop from the skies? No. Are they innate in the mind? No. They come from social practice, and from it alone. They come from three kinds of social practice: the struggle for production, the class struggle, and scientific experiment."

Sun Tzu lived in the later Spring and Autumn Period, a time when ancient Chinese society was changing from a slave to a feudal society. This was the time when there was fierce class struggle reflected in wars. Prior to this period, five *bo* [a title of nobility in ancient China equivalent to an earl]—Qi Yuan, Jin Wen, Qin Mu, Chu Zhuang, and Song Rang—were fighting for dominance, and the whole social system was in turbulence.

According to historical records for the early Spring and Autumn Period, there had been more than 130 small states fighting against one another. In the process, there emerged five powerful states: Qi, Jin, Qin, Chu, and Song (in fact, Song was not as strong as the others). They fought for overall control, bullying smaller and weaker states and invading their neighbors. During the period of about two hundred years before Sun Tzu lived, there had occurred three to four hundred wars among them. In addition to military struggles, which produced a diversified art of war, history had witnessed political struggles, economic struggles (reflected mainly in commercial relations and in the seizure of other states' wealth by economic practices), and diplomatic struggles (usually in alliances and counteralliances, and protection of smaller states in order to enlarge one's sphere of influence). *Sun Tzu's Art of War* was indeed a summary of the experiences of these wars. It is, therefore, still immortal over two thousand years after it was written as far as many of its principles are concerned.

*Sun Tzu's Art of War* seems to be speaking in abstract terms. But when we relate it to various wars that occurred before Sun

Tzu's time, things become clearer. Of course, it is not the intention of the author to link each and every principle of *Sun Tzu's Art of War* to an historic event. Only one or two examples are to be given to elaborate upon Sun Tzu's central ideas.

## THE ESTIMATE OF THE SITUATION

"Estimates," the first chapter of *Sun Tzu's Art of War,* appraises the role that preliminary calculations play in a war: "If the calculations made in the temple before a battle indicate victory, it is because careful calculations show that your conditions for a battle are more favorable than that of your enemy; if they indicate defeat, it is because careful calculations show that favorable conditions for a battle are fewer. With more careful calculations, one can win, with less one cannot. How much less chance of victory has one who makes no calculations at all! By this means, one can foresee the outcome of a battle."

The "preliminary calculations" in modern times mean the decisions made by the highest command before a war after meticulous analysis regarding various factors of war. One does not enter a war if one is not sure to win. That is to say, the decision as to whether to enter a war is the outcome of a comprehensive study beforehand of various factors of political and military experience, and of diplomacy and geography. The following example should suffice to show what is meant by this.

## The War of Cheng Pu

The War of Cheng Pu in 632 B.C. was one of fairly large scale during the Spring and Autumn Period. It was also a war enabling Jin Wen Gong to secure his position of dominance and it laid the foundation for the Jin state to be supreme among states for a long time. Before the war, the monarch of Jin and his officials carefully weighed various factors pertaining to both sides. *Zou Zhuan,* a book about Chinese history, has a very vivid description of the war as follows: "In winter, Chu and its followers besieged Sung. Gongsun Guru of Sung went to Jin for help."

Xian Zhen, one of the marshals in Jin, said: "This is the time for us to pay our debt of gratitude to Sung by coming to their rescue. It is also the time for us to obtain hegemony in the area."

Hu Yen, a Jin general, also remarked: "Chu secured the Cao state not long ago and it had matrimonial relations with the Wei state. If we attacked Cao and Wei, Chu was sure to come to their rescue. Then Qi and Sung would certainly be relieved of Sung's siege." Jin Wen Gong, the sovereign of Jin, followed their advice.

The next spring Jin's troops attacked Cao and Wei, and were victorious. But things turned out unexpectedly. Zi Yu, a senior general of Chu, continued the attack on the state of Sung, which again sent Man Yin to Jin to ask for emergency help.

During the discussion, Jin Wen Gong stated: "If we do not try our best to help Sung, it will break off relations with us. If Chu is not in a mood of reconciliation, we shall have to go to war against it. In that case, it is essential to get help from Qi and Qin. But what if they decline?"

Xian Zhen replied: "Tell Sung not to ask us but pay handsome tributes to Qi and Qin, and then ask them to plead with Chu. In the meantime, we, having kept the sovereign of Cao in captivity, will give a part of the territories of the Cao state and Wei state to Sung. Being closely allied with the two states, Chu will not tolerate it. Pleased with Sung's tributes and annoyed with Chu's stubbornness, Qi and Qin will certainly resort to arms with Chu."

## SUBDUING THE ENEMY
## WITHOUT A FIGHT

As we have already observed in *Sun Tzu's Art of War,* there are such important principles as: "to attack the enemy's strategy," "to disrupt enemy's alliances," and "to subdue the enemy without fighting." That is to say, in fighting a war one must first attack the enemy's strategy and disrupt his diplomacy in order to subdue his troops without fighting.

Sun Tzu was against fighting a reckless war in the field with the enemy. He stressed: "The next best is to attack the enemy's army and the worst policy is to attack a walled city." Both of these, he thought, should be done only when there is no alternative. This is really a wise remark of an experienced person in commanding battles. His conclusion was: "To subdue the enemy's troops without fighting is the supreme excellence."

Was this conclusion Sun Tzu's wishful thinking or was he just following his own inclinations? The answer is negative, because he came to this conclusion after summing up many war experiences in history.

*Zou Zhuan* recorded many outstanding military strategists who, with or without a powerful backup force, defeated a stronger enemy with the help of their wisdom, courage, insight, and eloquence. They achieved the aim of subduing the enemy without fighting. There were two well-known wars before Sun Tzu's time which proved that principle.

### The Battle Between Qi and Chu

In 656 B.C., Qi Huan Gong—allied with the states of Lu, Song, Chen, Wei, Zheng, Xu, and Cao—attacked the powerful Chu state in the south. Facing aggressive troops from all sides, Chu was obviously inferior in numbers.

The emperor of Chu sent an envoy to Qi, asking Qi Huan Gong: "You are in the north and we are in the south. We have nothing whatsoever to do with each other. What is the reason for your invading us, pray?"

Guan Zhong, a minister of the Qi state, instead of replying, brought the envoy to account for not paying tributes to Emperor Zhou (the common puppet monarch of all the states, in whose name Qi Huan Gong had launched the war against Chu). He also blamed Chu for the drowning of King Zhou Sao, which had already taken place a long time ago. The envoy of Chu admitted guilt in not paying tributes and promised to restore them soon, but denied any responsibility for King Zhou Sao's death. Qi was dissatisfied with the reply and continued its advance.

The sovereign of Chu sent another envoy, Qu Wan, to Qi to make further representations. While receiving the envoy, the sovereign of Qi purposefully asked his guards to create an impressive formation in an attempt to coerce Qu Wan into signing a treaty favorable to the state of Qi.

In a neither haughty nor humble manner, Qu Wan said: "Who dares to disobey you if you placate various sovereigns with virtue and morals? But if you intend to use force, Mount Fangcheng would be our city wall and the Hanshui River, our city moat [meaning that the city will be impregnable]. Even though you have a powerful army, it would be useless."

This was diplomatic language used with perfect assurance. Qi Huan Gong had to sign a peace treaty (not entirely favorable to Qi) with Chu and withdraw his troops. This example was significant in that Qi was powerful while Chu was gifted and just with its language. Both sides achieved their respective goals but the real winner was Chu.

In 579–546 B.C., there was an anti-war movement launched by Hua Yuan and Xiang Shu, two militarists of the weak Sung state, which serves as a good example of subduing an enemy without fighting. At that time, smaller states, like Zheng and Sung, sandwiched between the more powerful states of Jin and Chu, were often harassed. Zheng used to amass large numbers of slaves and jade and silk objects at the border, and give them as state gifts to whomever came to cause a skirmish. Sung suffered even more and, in one siege by Chu, its subjects had to swap their children to be eaten as food.

The anti-war movement was launched under this circumstance and was successful. Sung persuaded all the neighboring states (including Jin and Chu) to conclude a treaty with both Jin and Chu as leaders of the alliance.

The contents of the treaty included the provision: "Jin and Chu shall not use force against each other. They shall be bound by a common cause and go through thick and thin together. . . . Whoever breaks its pledge shall be struck dead by Heaven."

The treaty also stipulated that the smaller states should pay tributes to Jin and Chu. Apparently, it was better for them to give out some money and valuables than to suffer from calamities of war. After the signing of this treaty, there emerged among the states a situation of tranquility, particularly after the movement launched by Xiang Shu. For more than thirty years, there was no major war between them.

The above-mentioned events were just as familiar to Sun Tzu as the wars of the past hundred years are to us. He had as much knowledge of the antiwar drive launched by Xiang Shu as we do of the history of the two world wars in the twentieth century. Therefore, his doctrine that "the best way is to subdue an enemy without fighting" was based on historical fact.

## SUMMARY

As a whole, Sun Tzu attached great importance to employing politics, diplomacy, and strategic considerations for the purpose of subduing an enemy. To some extent, this was a strategy based on one's economic strength. Obviously, Sun Tzu was of the opinion that one should make the enemy yield by means of one's powerful political and diplomatic capability and economic and military strength rather than by means of war. In today's language, this is called a "policy backed by up strength," or strategy of nuclear deterrence. Sun Tzu was certainly the first person in world history to have put forward this doctrine.

# Chapter 9
# Naive Materialism and
# Primitive Dialectics

It is sometimes difficult to correctly appraise various occurrences in the world because of their differences in time, place, historical background, development, and end result. But it is often possible to prove the correctness of some relative truth from the success or failure of what has happened in accordance with the rule of historical development.

From a philosophical point of view, "materialism is man's practical knowledge of the objective world which has been developed on the basis of his social practice." It is praiseworthy for Sun Tzu to have written *The Art of War* by synthesizing different social phenomena (mainly related to war) more than two thousand years ago, and learning from books on the art of war written by his predecessors.

*Sun Tzu's Art of War* brings to light many common laws of war, discusses rather comprehensively factors leading to victory in a war, and reflects the thought of naive materialism and primitive dialectics.

During the Spring and Autumn Period, China was going through the transitional stage from slave society to feudal society. In the duration of its five hundred years, different schools of thought—developed by Confucius, Mencius, Yangzi, Mozi, Zhuangzi, Laozi, and Sun Tzu—spread widely. With the development of society, some of them died out, but some continued to spread. Sun Tzu's doctrine is among those which have been popular since then. This fully demonstrates its practical value.

*Sun Tzu's Art of War* contains thoughts of naive materialism and primitive dialectics that are reflected in many of his statements. The following are some of the obvious ones: "Thus, the reason the enlightened ruler and the wise general conquer the enemy whenever they strike and their achievements surpass those of ordinary men is foreknowledge. This foreknowledge cannot be elicited from spirits, nor from gods, nor by analogy with past events, nor from deductive calculations. It must be obtained from men who know the enemy situation." Sun Tzu did not believe in gods, spirits, or divination; nor did he rely upon astrology for his actions. It is the pride of our national culture that Sun Tzu was an atheist even more than two thousand years ago.

## ATHEISM VS. THEISM

There has been long rivalry between the two world outlooks—atheism and theism—and that has obviously been reflected in military affairs. We know from inscriptions on bones and tortoise shells of the Shang Dynasty and on bronze objects that in ancient times divination was frequently practiced in China before fighting to forecast the result of war.

In ancient times, there were debates between generals with materialist ideas and those who were superstitious over whether or not it was favorable to move troops on the day of Jiazi. The argument the former gave in refutation of the latter was that the Battle of Muye (1098 B.C.) was launched on the day of Jiazi. It was a victory for the King Zhou Wu and disaster for King Ying Zhou. This was a powerful argument.

In spite of the fact that Sun Tzu refuted superstitions, there still have been quite a few fatuous generals and commanders who practiced divination before moving troops. That has been so not only in China, but also in the West. About half a century before the Christian era, the Roman Julius Caesar was having a war with the Germanic people. In one of the battles, only half of the main force of the Germanic army was fighting. This resulted in a big victory for the Roman army, which would have surely been defeated if its enemy's main force had joined the fight. According to a statement made by a Germanic prisoner of war, the reason that the Germanic main force did not join the fight was because its leaders believed that the gods did not wish the Germanic army to fight before the crescent moon rose, or else they would suffer defeat.

All this illustrates how commendable Sun Tzu's materialistic thought of atheism was. His principle that "must be obtained from men who know the enemy situation" did not apply only to the use of spies. In fact, his emphasis upon the role of men was reflected in his exposition of political, diplomatic, and economic factors that bore upon a war. His materialistic doctrines reflected that the ruler should have "the people in harmony with them" and "calculations in temple." The enemy's strategies and alliances should be disrupted. "After one thousand pieces of gold are in hand, one hundred thousand troops may be raised."

## SUN TZU'S PRIMITIVE DIALECTICAL THOUGHT

There are also many statements in *Sun Tzu's Art of War* that reflect his primitive dialectical thought. We can easily pick out some of his remarks that are in accord with the law of the unity of opposites. For example: extraordinary and normal, void and actuality, circuitous and straight, strong and weak, victorious and defeated, favorable and unfavorable, enemy and oneself, numerous and scanty, fatigued and at ease, well fed and hungry, turbulence and peace, noisy and quiet, advance and retreat, far and near, gain and loss, and brave and cowardly.

While expounding on void and actuality, he held that there must be void in actuality and vice versa. In the chapter entitled "Posture of Army," he wrote: "In battle there are only the normal and extraordinary forces, but their combinations are limitless; none can comprehend them all." And he added: "To ensure your army will sustain the enemy's attack without suffering defeat is a matter of operating the extraordinary and the normal forces. . . . For these two forces are mutually reproductive; their interaction as endless as that of interlocked rings. Who can determine where one ends and the other begins?"

He strongly maintained that one must consider both favorable and unfavorable factors while making judgments. He pointed out in the chapter entitled "The Nine Variables": "The wise general in his deliberations must consider both favorable and unfavorable factors. By taking into account the favorable factors, he makes his plan feasible; by taking into account the unfavorable, he may resolve the difficulties."
He again pointed out in the chapter "Maneuvering": "Those skilled in war avoid the enemy when its spirit is keen, and

attack it when it is sluggish and the soldiers are homesick. This is control of the moral factor. In good order, they await an enemy in disorder; in serenity, an enemy in clamorousness. This is control of the mental factor. Close to the field of battle, they await an enemy coming from afar; at rest, they await an exhausted enemy; with well-fed troops, they await a hungry enemy. This is control of the physical factor. They do not engage an enemy advancing with well-ordered banners, nor one whose formations are in impressive array. This is control of the factor of changing circumstances."

From the above-mentioned doctrines of Sun Tzu, it can be seen that he was full of dialectical ideas in line with the universal law of unity of opposites.

In exploring Sun Tzu's theories, we also find that his thinking was systematic and objective. Judging from the way in which he looked at the nature and law of the world, his logical thinking was quite rigorous and, therefore, worthy of esteem.

# Chapter 10
# Universal Laws of War

Sun Tzu pointed out in the chapter entitled "Use of Spies": "Thus, the reason the enlightened ruler and the wise general conquer the enemy whenever they strike is foreknowledge." Foreknowledge, in essence, means to know the situation of the enemy and of yourself before the war starts, just as Sun Tzu wrote in the chapter entitled "Offensive Strategy": "Know the enemy and know yourself; in a hundred battles, you will never be defeated. When you are ignorant of the enemy but know yourself, your chances of winning or losing are equal. If ignorant both of the enemy and of yourself, you are sure to be defeated in every battle." No commanders—whether in modern or ancient times, in China or abroad—can afford to ignore this principle.

It is a universal law which is without parallel in history, and it represents the best of Sun Tzu's thought. Philosophically, it belongs to naive materialism. From the point of view of war theory, it is a fundamental law of making judgment and analysis. And from the viewpoint of directing a war, it constitutes an important choice of first looking for conditions that may lead to victory and then for opportunities that would lead to a sure victory.

## MODERN INTELLIGENCE GATHERING

The funds that the Soviet Union and the United States spent on intelligence gathering for the purpose of knowing each other's dealings were enormous. One United States general who had been in charge of intelligence work pointed out that since the end of World War II, the U.S. had spent no less than $50 to $75 billion on the establishment of an intelligence system. He added that in spite of this, the U.S. was in no better a position than it was before the invasion of Pearl Harbor in 1941. This statement was made in the 1970s. Today one can well imagine how high the intelligence expenses are. As for the Soviet Union, it keeps its defense expenses top secret, but it is not difficult to infer how much money it spends on its intelligence work.

Mao Zedong highly appreciated Sun Tzu's principle, saying that it remains a scientific truth today. In addition, he pointed out in his essay, "Problems of Strategy in China's Revolutionary War": "Some people are good at knowing themselves and poor at knowing their enemy, and some are the other way around; neither can solve the problem of learning and applying the laws of war. There is a saying in the book of Sun Tzu, the great military scientist of ancient China, 'Know the enemy and know yourself, and in a hundred battles you will never be defeated,' which refers both to the stage of learning and to the stage of application, both to knowing the laws of the development of objective reality and to deciding on our own action in accordance with these laws in order to overcome the enemy facing us. We should not take this saying lightly."

Let us examine the theoretical principles of practical significance in *The Art of War* from three aspects—political, economic, and the art of direction.

## THE POLITICAL ASPECT

Quite a few problems Sun Tzu discussed about war fall within the political sphere. For example, he said: "War is a matter of vital importance to the state; a matter of life or death; the road either to survival or to ruin. Hence, it is imperative that it be studied thoroughly. Therefore, appraise it in terms of the five fundamental factors and make comparisons of various conditions of the enemy and yourself when seeking the outcome of war. The first of the fundamental factors is politics; the second, weather; the third, terrain; the fourth; the commander; and the fifth, doctrine." "What is of supreme importance in war is to attack the enemy's strategy; next best is to disrupt the enemy's alliances."

Most of these statements involve political activities before or during a war. All these doctrines had never been and could never be put forward systematically before Sun Tzu's time. He systematically brought military actions into the political arena. By politics, he meant the ways to cause the people to be in harmony with their ruler. That is to say, the ruler has to impose his will upon the people and only in so doing can he succeed in making the people accompany him in war and peace without fear of mortal peril. In other words, only when political harmony is achieved can it be possible to defeat the enemy. By the commander, he meant the ability and qualities which a commander should have. And by doctrine, he meant the military organization, system, and regulations. In short, three of the five factors are directly connected with politics. Among the seven elements he mentioned, the first, second, fourth, fifth, and seventh are directly related to politics—namely, which ruler is wiser and more able, which commander is the more talented, in which army regulations and instructions are better carried out, which troops are the stronger, and which side administers rewards and punishments in a more enlightened manner.

Sun Tzu was one of the first persons in ancient China who believed that diplomacy was one of the keys to the outcome of war. In military works before Sun Tzu, there had been similar discussions about the importance of diplomacy, but none had summarized it into theory as Sun Tzu did.

Sun Tzu discussed the relationships between war and politics, and from there, he proceeded to the gravity, cruelty, and disruptiveness of war. He pointed out: "When the army engages in protracted campaigns, the resources of the state will fall short. When your weapons are dulled and ardor dampened, your strength exhausted and treasure spent, the chieftains of neighboring states will take advantage of your crisis to act. In that case, no man, however wise, will be able to avert the disastrous consequences that ensue."

It is true that Sun Tzu was not able to formulate the scientific principles: "War is the continuation of politics," "Politics is war without bleeding," or "War is politics with bleeding," but he was clearly aware that whether you will be victorious or defeated, much depends upon whether your government is honest and upright and your system is good. He wrote as a conclusion in the chapter "Dispositions": "Those skilled in war cultivate politics, preserve the laws and institutions, and are therefore able to formulate victorious policies." It is commendable for Sun Tzu as a military commander to have been aware of the important effect that politics has on war.

Karl von Clausewitz stated: "War is the continuation of politics." This well-known dictum has been understood in the West to be an insightful remark. Now it has been found that a similar remark was made in an ancient Chinese writing, *The Strategy of Warring States,* as early as the Qin Dynasty. It explicitly stated: "It is impossible to gain profit without making efforts and to extend one's territory by sitting idly. Even the five emperors and three kings could not achieve that. The only way to attain that goal is to continue doing it through war." Obviously, gaining profits and extending one's territory are both political aims. One has to achieve them through war.

In *The Art of War,* written by Sun Bin, excavated from the Yin Que Mountains, it is recorded: "It is impossible for a sovereign whose prestige and ability are not comparable to the five emperors and three kings to carry out a policy of humanity, justice, and virtue, and be a model of civility. This was, in fact, yearned for by Yao and Shun [legendary monarchs and sages in ancient China], but found to be impossible. One had to solve certain problems by force." This is tantamount to achieving a political aim through war.

## THE ECONOMIC ASPECT

Before we discuss Sun Tzu's idea concerning the effects of economics upon war, it is necessary for us to quote relevant passages from *Guan Zi,* a book published one century earlier than Sun Tzu's, which reflects Guan Zhong's thought on military economics, in order to have a better understanding of military theories in ancient China.

In the book *Guan Zi*, it is written: "If the state is wealthy, it will not be short of supplies even if the war lasts long; if the state has excellent weapons, it will not be exhausted after repeated attacks. If the army has any important matter, it is weapons. If it is not well equipped, you are giving away your troops for nothing. If you fight for one year, ten years' accumulation will be exhausted. An all-out war will exhaust all you have." All this means that it is difficult to fight a war without ample funds and excellent weapons.

Sun Tzu also attached great importance to relations between military actions and economics. He wrote: "In operations of war—when one thousand fast four-horse chariots, one thousand heavy chariots, and one thousand mail-clad soldiers are required; when provisions are transported for a thousand *li*; when there are expenditures at home and at the front, and stipends for entertainment of envoys and advisers—the cost of materials such as glue and lacquer, and of chariots and armor, will amount to one thousand pieces of gold a day. One hundred thousand troops may be dispatched only when this money is in hand. . . . If you fight with such a big army, a speedy victory is required. If victory is long delayed, troops will be exhausted and morale depressed. When troops attack cities, their strength will be exhausted."

He added: "Those skilled in war do not require a second

levy nor more than two provisions. They carry military equipment from the homeland, but rely on the enemy for provisions. Thus, the army is plentifully provided with food."

"When a country is impoverished by military operations, it is because of distant transportation; carrying supplies for great distances renders the people destitute. Where troops are gathered, prices go up. When prices rise, the wealth of the people is drained away. When wealth is drained away, the peasantry will be afflicted with urgent exactions. With this loss of wealth and exhaustion of strength, the households in the central plains will be extremely poor and seven-tenths of their wealth dissipated. As to government expenditures, those due to broken-down chariots, worn-out horses, armor and helmets, bows and arrows, spears and shields, protective mantlets, draft oxen, and wagons will amount to 60 percent of the total."

It is clear that Sun Tzu set great store by economics, namely, the financial situation of a country. His principle of fighting a speedy battle to force a quick decision originated from this idea. He believed that prolonged war was something that exhausted the wealth of a country. If financial resources dried up, additional taxes would be levied on people; as a result, the homes of the people would be stripped bare. This vicious cycle would lead to attacks from neighboring states. In this case, "No man, however wise, will be able to avert the consequences that ensue."

Sun Tzu was quite practical and realistic. While discussing relationships between war and economics, he emphasized the use of resources and manpower of the enemy state. He wrote: "One *zhong* [a measurement in ancient China] of the enemy's provisions is equivalent to twenty of one's own; one *shi* [a weight in old China, approximately 60 kilograms] of the enemy's fodder to twenty *shi* of one's own." He strongly maintained that one should offer big rewards to one's soldiers and treat the captives well. One should utilize the captured weapons, military materials, and prisoners of war to replenish one's own troops in order to support the war. These ideas of his were progressive ones of the new emerging feudal class.

During the war of liberation in China, several millions of Jiang Jieshi troops were captured by the PLA and became its staunch fighters after political education. As for the amount of weapons captured from the enemy, including tanks, cannons, warships, and airplanes, it was unprecedented at home and abroad. This he called "winning a battle and becoming stronger."

Compared with wars in ancient times, the dependence of modern wars on economics is far greater. Even the powerful and financially secure United States felt it difficult to cope with a protracted war in Vietnam. General Westmoreland, the American commander in chief in Vietnam, quoted Sun Tzu as his argument for withdrawing his troops: "There has never been a protracted war from which a country has benefited."

Therefore, it is clear that the more modernized an army is, the more dependent it is on economics. Sun Tzu's doctrine about relationships between war and economics has not lost its significance with the passage of time.

## THE ART OF DIRECTION

We have discussed problems of war from the strategic point of view in previous chapters. In this section, we will approach it from the tactical side—in other words, from the aspect of the art of directing a war. (Sun Tzu made no clear distinction between strategy and direction in his thirteen chapters.) Discussion about the art of direction appeared in several chapters in *Sun Tzu's Art of War*. However, here we will limit it to two aspects: initiative and flexibility.

### Initiative

How does one have the initiative? This is the primary question to answer while discussing the art of direction. If you lose the initiative in the battlefield, you will be thrown into passivity and be attacked at all times. Sun Tzu's idea of maintaining the initiative was primarily reflected in his doctrines "to bring the enemy to the battlefield and be not brought there by him" and "a victorious army tries to create conditions for victory before seeking battle." All wise generals should try their best to utilize these ideas.

Sun Tzu advocated: "A skillful commander takes up a position in which he cannot be defeated and seizes every opportunity to win over his enemy. Thus, a victorious army tries to create conditions for victory before seeking battle; an army destined to be defeated fights in the hope of gaining victory by sheer luck." "Generally, he who comes to the battlefield first and awaits his enemy is at ease; he who comes later and rushes into the fight is weary. And, therefore, those skilled in war bring the enemy to the field of battle and are not brought there by him."

It is a truth that one should try to impose one's will on the enemy. And only when you take up a position in which you cannot be defeated—in other words, you have the initiative in hand—can you take measures to move enemy troops and lead them to defeat.

When you first occupy a favorable position in the battlefield, you can move enemy troops and transform the conditions between the enemy and yourself, just as Sun Tzu advised. All military scientists, ancient or contemporary, Chinese or foreign, know that war is a contest of strength, and strength can be transformed. When the sides are evenly matched (or even if the enemy is stronger), if we have the initiative, the situation can be transformed. If we are able to tire the enemy who is at ease, we shall succeed in obtaining a favorable situation in which we can await the enemy.

Early in the twentieth century, the Baltic fleet of Tzarist Russia was totally annihilated during the Russian-Japanese War. The victory was achieved—according to Marshal Togo Heihachiro, the Japanese commander of this sea battle—due to the application of Sun Tzu's doctrine "to wait at one's ease for an exhausted enemy." It was true that Russia's Baltic fleet committed a disastrous mistake by sailing all the way to the Far East, exhausting its sailors, while the Japanese navy was waiting for them at its ease.

The Baltic Sea was tens of thousands of kilometers away from the Sea of Japan. Furthermore, the Russian fleet was not in a position to reach the Far East by passing through the British-controlled Strait of Gibraltar, and then going through the Mediterranean Sea and the Suez Canal, because Britain was an ally of Japan. It had to go around the Cape of Good Hope, an additional voyage of over ten thousand kilometers.

In addition, after the Baltic fleet crossed the Malacca Strait, the Japanese army spread false information (in accordance with Sun Tzu's doctrine, "War is based on deception") to the effect that the Japanese navy was ready to launch a surprise attack upon the Tzarist fleet in the South China Sea. Being taken in, the Baltic fleet had to sail all the time in combat readiness, which added to its weariness, and the seamen were totally exhausted when they reached the Tsushima Strait.

The Japanese navy had been waiting at ease and, therefore, won an unprecedented victory over the Russian fleet.

## Flexibility

Moving troops flexibly is another important principle in *Sun Tzu's Art of War*. He advocated: "Just as water has no constant shape, there are in warfare no constant conditions. Thus, one able to win victory by modifying his tactics in accordance with the enemy situation may be said to be divine." He added that moving troops should be like the snakes of Mount Chang which respond simultaneously: "When struck on the head, its tail attacks; when struck on the tail, its head attacks; when struck in the center, both head and tail attack."

In short, he maintained that one should adapt to the enemy's situation, and he opposed rigid tactics and mechanical materialism in war. He was also opposed to using outmoded methods. He was in favor of using normal and extraordinary forces, the solid and the void, the true and the false interchangeably, in order to confuse the enemy and obtain victory.

For the sake of carrying out his own propositions, Sun Tzu often tried to occupy a position of initiative and take preemptive measures. He pointed out: "Speed is the essence of war. Take advantage of the enemy's unpreparedness, make your way by unexpected routes, and attack the enemy where he is unguarded." It was because of these flexible tactics that he could keep the enemy units from uniting, cooperating, and supporting each other.

A commander should be very clear about the field situation and learn an art of direction with which he can manipulate the enemy. Sun Tzu wrote: "One who is skilled at making the enemy move does so by creating a situation, according to which the enemy will act; he entices the enemy with something he is certain to take. He keeps the enemy on the move by holding out bait and then attacks him with picked troops."

With regard to manipulating the enemy, there is an incisive statement in the chapter entitled "Void and Actuality": "Analyze the enemy's plans so that you will know his short-comings as well as strong points. Agitate him in order to ascertain the pattern of his movement. Lure him out to reveal his dispositions and ascertain his position. Launch a probing attack in order to learn where his strength is abundant and where deficient." In this way, he can achieve what Sun Tzu said: "His offensive will be irresistible if he makes for his enemy's weak positions; he cannot be overtaken when he withdraws, if he moves swiftly. . . . When I wish to give battle, my enemy, even though protected by high walls and deep moats, cannot help but engage me, for I attack a position he must relieve. When I wish to avoid fighting, I may defend myself simply by drawing a line on the ground; the enemy will be unable to attack me because I divert him from going where he wishes."

If you can move as flexibly as Sun Tzu described, you can certainly dominate the battlefield. "Thus, I say that victory can be achieved. For even if the enemy is numerically stronger, I can prevent him from engaging."

The essence of using troops flexibly is the principle: "War is based on deception." It is stated in the chapter entitled "Estimates": "All warfare is based on deception. Therefore, when capable of attacking, feign incapacity; when active in moving troops, feign inactivity; when near the enemy, make it appear that you are far away; when far away, make it seem that you are near." It all shows flexibility to be capable or incapable, active or inactive, far away or near. For instance, the principle that "when far away, make it seem that you are near" means that you should try to maneuver near the enemy in order to confuse him when you are actually moving troops at a faraway place.

The following are two examples showing two famous generals' (one ancient and the other contemporary) success in using this principle.

### Han's Campaign Against Chu

In 205 B.C., Han Xin (of the Han state) wanted to attack Wei Wangbao (of the Chu state) across the Yellow River. Han's intention was to attack Wei from the rear at Anyi (in the present Anyi County, Shan Xi Province), from faraway Xiayang (in the present Hanchen, Shan Xi Province). But he created a diversion by collecting materials for crossing the Yellow River at a nearby place called Linjing as if he planned to cross the river there. Wei Wangbao was taken in by the action and deployed his main force along Linjing, and Anyi was left unguarded. Consequently, Han Xin's troops crossed the river at Xiayang without resistance. This was one of the main campaigns between the Chu and Han states.

### The Invasion of Normandy

In the European landing operation during World War II, U.S. General Eisenhower decided that the Allied forces should land at Normandy in the northwest of France. But he hinted that the troops were going to land at the Calais area by the visible movement of army, navy, and air forces, and by establishing a headquarters in that area. Eisenhower also had false information spread and a sham telegram sent in order to confuse Hitler. As a result, Nazi Germany was fooled and concentrated its main force along the Calais area. Finally, the Allied forces landed at Normandy successfully.

### Mao Zedong's Emphasis on Initiative and Flexibility

In his military writings, Mao Zedong also stressed the important role that initiative and flexibility play in a war. He compared initiative to an army's freedom of action: "Freedom of action is the very life of an army and, once it is lost, the army is close to defeat or destruction." He also made brilliant observations on flexibility: "Flexibility consists in the intelligent commander's ability to take timely and appropriate measures on the basis of objective conditions after 'judging the hour and sizing up the situation' (including the enemy's situation, our situation, and the terrain), and this flexibility is 'ingenuity in varying tactics.'"

It is entirely practical to examine Sun Tzu's theory with this yardstick. There is a large amount of practical theory discussed with regard to the art of direction in *Sun Tzu's Art of War*. Only notable ideas have been discussed in this writing.

# Chapter 11
# Obsolete Ideas in
# Sun Tzu's Art of War

Truth develops constantly with the progress of times. Mao
Zedong pointed out in his writing *On Practice*: "The movement of change in the world of objective reality is neverend-
ing and so is man's cognition of truth through practice."
Keeping this in mind while evaluating *Sun Tzu's Art of War*, a correct conclusion can be reached.

Generally speaking, when ancient academic works are
assessed, it is not wrong to affirm or negate something by say-

ing: "Because of limitations of times and class. . . ." But it seems to provide the readers with a deeper understanding of the ancient work if it is appraised with an eye to the background in which it was written.

The main shortcomings of *Sun Tzu's Art of War* are that it does not discuss the nature of war. According to the statistics gathered by historians, there occurred approximately four to five hundred big or small wars during the Spring and Autumn Period when Sun Tzu lived. Mencius, a famous scholar who lived some time later than Sun Tzu, made a widely acknowledged conclusion: "There were no just wars during the Spring and Autumn Period." Is this conclusion correct? The answer is negative.

The wars between the big powers during that period were definitely unjust, but those launched by smaller nations against the aggression of big powers were quite another matter. For instance, Sung, a small state, was besieged by two big powers, Jin and Chu, and its people had to exchange their children with one another to be eaten as food. Was not Sung on the just side when it fought against the aggressors?

In the history book *Zou Zhuan*, there were accounts of many uprisings by serfs from the seventh to sixth century B.C. Famous among them were the insurrection of serfs in Qi against the construction of city walls, and the rebellion of serfs in Zhen against the ruling class. Were the serfs not on the just side when they rose against oppression of the ruling class and the serf owners as a result of intensification of class contradictions? Unfortunately, this is not considered in *Sun Tzu's Art of War*. This could not but be regarded as an outstanding shortcoming and a policy of keeping the soldiers in ignorance.

This obscurantist policy was a flaw in Sun Tzu's work. No doubt, he wrote: "Regard your soldiers as your children" and "Command them with civility but keep them under control by iron discipline." It seems that he was propagating concern for soldiers and attention to discipline in the army. But what he did during the war was quite the opposite. He went so far as to maintain that the commander "should be capable of keeping his officers and men in ignorance of his plans. . . . He drives his men now in one direction, now in another, like a shepherd driving a flock of sheep, and none knows where he is going. . . . The business of a general is to kick away the ladder behind soldiers when they have climbed up a height." All these can be said to be reactionary ideas of looking down upon the laboring people.

The second shortcoming is that he overemphasized the function of generals. He stated: "The general who understands how to employ troops is the minister of the people's fate and arbiter of the nation's destiny." Related to this was another view of his: "There are occasions when the commands of the sovereign need not be obeyed." There have been quite a few generals who, affected by this view, used it as a pretext for not obeying orders from the supreme command. Is this view correct? Since there has been war by mankind, it has always been conditioned by politics, and has never and in no way departed from politics. Therefore, it often causes irremediable damage to the nation if long-term and overall interests of the state are given up for the sake of local interests in the battlefield.

It is argued that in ancient times communications were poor and difficult and situations at the front changed quickly, so commanders had to act arbitrarily in order to cope with the changing situation. Tenable as the argument might be, the situation today has greatly changed. Nowadays, with the help of telecommunication, television, and man-made satellites, the supreme command has every small change in the battlefield at its fingertips. It is, therefore, entirely in a position to readjust its deployment or tactics in accordance with the new situation. A commander is in no way allowed to disobey orders from the supreme command for local interest. As a common rule of war, Sun Tzu's principle, "There are occasions when the commands of the sovereign need not be obeyed," is now obsolete.

## SUN TZU'S CONTRADICTIONS

The third point is that some of his principles are too rigid and mechanical. For example: "Do not thwart an army which is returning homewards. One must leave a way of escape to a surrounded enemy, and do not press a desperate enemy too hard." These principles are contradictory to many others in *Sun Tzu's Art of War* itself. For instance, consider his advice to ". . . avoid the enemy when its spirit is keen and attack it when it is sluggish and the soldiers are homesick." It is just the opposite of the former ones mentioned. The latter principle is, without a shadow of doubt, the correct one.

Sun Tzu suggested in the chapter entitled "Offensive Strategy" to surround an enemy when you are ten to his one. This is the idea of the "war of annihilation," which is certainly correct. Of course, you should not leave a way of escape to the enemy if you surround him. During the Huai-Hai campaign, if the PLA had left an outlet for the enemy to flee, it would have been as if it let the tiger return to the mountains. In that case, how could the PLA have achieved the victory of totally wiping out the enemy forces? The view that "one must leave a way of escape to a surrounded enemy" is considered too rigid because of the word "must." It can also be feasible or even advantageous to leave an outlet free for the enemy in case one wants to wind up the campaign speedily or to lure the enemy to fall into an ambush.

As for the doctrine to "not press a desperate enemy too hard," it is simply ludicrous. Mao Zedong had two very famous verses in one of his poems, which read:

With power and to spare we must pursue the tottering foe;

And not ape Xiang Yu the Conqueror seeking idle fame.

*Sun Tzu's Art of War* is a military work written more than two thousand years ago. However, many of its doctrines, principles, and rules are still of practical and universal significance. Therefore, it remains a valuable asset for the Chinese people and will remain so in any future war against aggression.

# Index

# Notes